BUTTERFLIES AND SHINY THINGS

A WOMEN'S GUIDE ON HOW TO MANAGE FINANCIAL DISTRACTIONS

JENNIFER WOODBECK THOMPSON

JENNIFER WOODBECK

BUTTERFLIES AND SHINY THINGS

A WOMEN'S GUIDE ON HOW TO MANAGE FINANCIAL DISTRACTIONS

JENNIFER WOODBECK THOMPSON

JENNIFER WOODBECK

Legal Disclaimer

Publisher
Connect with *Magnetic Entrepreneur Inc*
https://www.facebook.com/magneticentrepreneur
www.linkedin.com/in/magneticentrepreneur
E-Mail: info@magneticentrepreneurinc.com

ACKNOWLEDGEMENTS

Thank you to my darling husband, Patrick Thompson. You are my biggest cheerleader, and you always make me feel special. You have a unique way of promoting me to everyone you meet, and I am forever grateful to have you in my life. You have helped me raise our two amazing boys, Preston Woodbeck and Calvin Thompson. Preston, you are a shining star in my world. You have so much love to share, and you always expect people to be the best they can be. You changed my world the moment you were born and made me a proud momma at that moment and every day since. Calvin, you are amazingly special. You have a gift for making anyone smile, you have an infectious laugh, and you always strive for people to be happy. You arrived with a bang, and you have never stopped. You run everywhere you go and keep on running. I have so much gratitude for having these three boys in my life.

To my parents, I am sorry for all the things I did to stress you, haha. I know my adventures sometimes caused you to worry, but I have learned so much in my life, and I am grateful you let me spread my butterfly wings and explore. Mom and Roy, I am thankful for all the love and support you have given us and your help with watching Preston and Calvin. They love their time with both of you playing chess, board games, swimming in the lake, and baking. Dad, your constant concern and worry for my family and me help me to be a more caring person. Thank you for being honest with me and being a rock in our lives. I am truly lucky to have the best parents in the world. Your honesty, support, and occasional tough love have helped me to be the woman I am today.

Kathleen, Dave, Lily and Alex Wright, you are so important to me. Kathleen, I am so lucky to have spent my life with you as my sister, and I am so proud of you. Dave, I can't thank you enough for always being there for me, answering my questions, and sometimes laughing at the fun ideas I come up with. Kathleen and Dave, you are so blessed to have Lily and Alex. My niece and nephew are so fun and loving, and I always look forward to hearing their stories and adventures. Lily and Alex, I love you.

Sharon Aylward, you have been in my life for over 20 years, and I am grateful for all you have done. You welcomed me into your home when I moved back to Thunder Bay, you helped take of Preston when he was a newborn and you spent time teaching me about business and the importance of enjoying the things you love, such as gold, diamonds, and Arizona flee markets.

Thank you to my large extended family, Barry and Marilyn Gural, Candyce Gural, Curtis Gural & Sherry Scott, and Molly and Beatrice Gural, Carol Scott, Gary and Lavette Woodbeck, Erin Woodbeck, Matthew,

Melanie and Clara Woodbeck. We have spent a lifetime together laughing, taking trips, and cheering each other on. I am so lucky to have grown up with so many fun cousins. Michelle Tracz, Mike and Amy Tracz, Jason and Natasha Shack, Anna Marie and Victoria Eckensweiler, Shane and Jessica Keegan, I absolutely love my extra-extended family. You always felt like my blood relatives, and always included my family as your own. A special thank you to Auntie Michelle for always helping with Preston and Calvin when they were young, and we needed to work. You are so wonderful.

Loads of love to Lynn Kryskow, Jordan Kryskow, Pete and Katelin Middaugh; you took us in when we needed help the most. Auntie Lynn, I loved bringing you home a Whopper after my shift at Burger King. You always stayed up waiting for me with a smile. My pumpkin, Katelin, you were my first 'baby.' I loved you like you were mine, and loved carrying you around. I am so happy to see the beautiful, loving wife and mother you have become. Jordan, you are so hardworking and, although I don't get to see you very much, I know you have become a wonderful guy.

I absolutely adore my in-laws. Ron Thompson, Bill and Liz Kent, Jeff Thompson, Lori, Alex, and Kristen Thompson, Lana, Joe, Sam and Maya Allen, you all made me feel so welcome in your family from the first time we met. Well, I do think it also helped that the first time I met all of you, we also told you we were pregnant, and you were stuck with me. All kidding aside, even though we live very far apart, you are all so close to us. I appreciate all the trips you have made to celebrate our special moments in life, as well as just to visit for fun. My kids love spending time and hearing from each of you. As a momma, I appreciate all the effort you make, even though you are far away. Brian, Charmaine, Arleigh, and Nicole Hack, I appreciate all you have done to help with our move and, of course, welcoming us into your family. I am so grateful to get to know each of you over the past couple of years.

Paige Grant, Amber and Chris Maclean, Will Moore, and Matt Woods, what a rollercoaster the years have been, and I have loved every second of it because I have had all of you in it. I wouldn't be where I am today if Amber and her sassiness didn't spend the time with me that fateful afternoon at Kelsey's. Amber, I am forever grateful that you introduced me to this world of finance. You taught me so much, and I knew I could always count on your help. You have become such an incredible friend along the way also. Chris, you are my favourite travelling roommate. I love our chats, and especially that you don't really chat with many other people, it makes it even more special. You are such a loving and devoted husband to Amber, and I see how much you love each other. Thank you, Will and Matt, for always having my back, being my rocks, and also being jokers with me. We can always be serious when needed and goofballs the rest of the time; you two are so special to me. Paige, thank you for being you. We may not always have seen eye to eye on things outside of work, but I adore your ethics, determination, and ability to make anyone feel special. You care so much about people and helping them to be the best version of themselves. You see something unique in people, even if they don't see it, and that makes you unique also. Don't ever change!

I am very grateful to RJ and Chelsea Johnson. You have both welcomed me into your work family before I was even part of it. RJ, you always answer when I call and are willing to help me learn more. I respect and value your opinion foremost. You expand my vision and push me to be the better every day. You are a wealth of knowledge and experience, and I look forward to years of your mentorship. Chelsea, you are a huge support to my business, as well as a friend. Thank you for always being the woman behind the scenes who is in the know and on the ball. I look forward to a long relationship with both of you. You have built something amazing in your business and your family. Way to go!

To some of my amazing friends, Darren and Heidi Henderson, Dr. Bella and Sean Irwin, Cari Kruzel and Keith Cochrane, Rochelle and Tyler Lee, Grant and Linda Stevens, Shawn Talbot, Ranji Agarwal, Meaghan Sharp, Catherine Tombs, you have all laughed and cried with me and also supported me as I made major changes in life. Your true friends are the ones that stick around when your life goes through rough times.

I spent 17 years working in healthcare and spent the last ten years working with some great people. Shelley Prevost, Maureen Dillon, Tina Poulin, Dr. Cheryl Everall, Dr. Anna Laakso, some fabulous nurses on the 2nd floor, and the great physio team on 2 south, you all hold special places in my life. Shelley, you were in my initial interview, and I was so impressed with your passion for chronic ventilation and lung health. I have learned so much from you over the years and appreciate that you always pushed for 120%. You taught me to expect more and always do more. Maureen and Tina, I had so much fun in pulmonary rehab with both of you. You both greet everyone with a smile and instantly make people feel at home. Dr. Everall and Dr. Laakso, thank you for your trust and support in me and for becoming friends first. You valued and respected my opinion as I did yours, a true patient care team. To the nurses and physio team, we had lots of laughs, and I appreciate that you always included me as part of your team. I met so many amazing patients and families, and will always hold them dear to my heart. As a team, we fought battles together and lost some, but we always pulled together. I appreciate all I learned in healthcare and the friendships I made.

Raymond Aaron and Shiraz Baboo, I appreciate you introducing me to the idea of writing this book. I always knew I had a bigger vision, but didn't know how I was going to share it with more people. You showed me how to be available to so many more. Thank you for all you do and the support you give to people like me.

Ed Mylett and Jaime Villalovos, I appreciate you. I'm grateful you share so much of yourself and bring a positive impact on the world. You continue to bring light to others, as well as share your expertise.

Sonia Stringer, thank you for being the first person to really believe in my ability to influence others. You showed me to magic words and to always be a resource, not a sales pitch. My ability to talk to people and learn from others improved thanks to your guidance.

I am truly lucky for all the friendships, experiences and leadership that I have had so far in my life, and I know there will be many more.

TESTIMONIALS

Even prior to meeting with Jennifer to go over my finances, I was really looking forward to it. She did not disappoint. She really made me feel excited to talk about my money instead of dreading that topic in general, so it was really reassuring to meet with her. I felt weightless by the time we were done!

M. O'Quinn, Toronto, Ontario

I am very thankful to have had Jennifer advise me about my finances this past year. Taking control over how I invest, what my retirement plans are, and leaving adequate insurance for my children has been the best form of self-care I could have asked for. Working together, we made adjustments to my account or made withdrawals to cover unforeseen expenses and focused, as a team, on what my needs were. Jennifer really took the fear out of financial planning and replaced it with trust. My only wish was that I had done it sooner!

Joanne Valley, Thunder Bay, Ontario

Jenn is a kind, professional and knowledgeable woman, helping families get into better financial shape, one family at a time!

Sarah Phelan, St. Catharines, Ontario

TABLE OF CONTENTS

Table of Contents

FOREWORD

In this time of Covid-19 with world-wide financial uncertainty, job losses and economic challenges, Jennifer Woodbeck Thompson's book on gaining personal financial control couldn't have come at a more opportune time.

Jennifer starts with a feminine perspective that women have different views on money and later how women's secret obsessions affect their decisions on what is important in this realm.

The title *Butterflies and Shiny Things - A Women's Guide On How To Manage Financial Distractions* is part of that outlook that demonstrates the types of things that can affect a woman's choice of action.

Attention is drawn not only to the basics of mindset, goal setting, a financial needs analysis, budgeting, saving, credit, insurance, retirement and investing, but Jennifer gives tips and tricks to plan and execute your vision to accomplish your goals.

Jennifer also goes into the technical terminology and details of important concepts surrounding financial investment vehicles and their benefits and drawbacks. In addition, she relates the historical issues with women and finance and gives legal landmark decisions which changed the ability of women to direct their financial future.

This comprehensive guide is so well written that it is easy to understand and conveys the message in an encouraging and light-hearted manner. Even subjects like mortgages are fully explained, with the various kinds detailed, so the reader has a clear understanding that there is a wide choice, depending on the desired outcome.

Every woman, young or old, married or single, will benefit from this guide, especially in the area of saving, where Jennifer shows the advantages of starting early with charts that point out the blunt facts and dollar differences of various strategies.

Jennifer's experience in the financial field makes this book, *Butterflies and Shiny Things - A Women's Guide On How To Manage Financial Distractions*, a credible and valued resource for all women.

- Robert J. Moore
5x International Best-Selling Author
CEO of Magnetic Entrepreneur Inc.™
Guinness World Record Holder

WHY EVERY WOMAN NEEDS TO KNOW THIS

People grow through experience if they meet life honestly and courageously.

This is how character is built.

- Eleanor Roosevelt, American First Lady

We all have those moments when the problem in our lives feels so overwhelming that we just want to bow down in defeat. Those are the moments where you stand tall and refuse to allow yourself to. You say "No" to what you want in life. No one is stopping you from living your best life. It may seem that way, but the power to change your life resides within you. It's common for women to avoid what they want in life in order to please someone else. You can have the life you want and make others happy. Just remember making yourself happy matters too. Why not have both?

In this book, I'm going to help you to understand the concepts of money and finance in an entertaining and easy way. Before we get to that though, let me tell you a little about my life, my struggles, and how they led me to writing this book for you.

Parents' Success and Struggle

At the time of writing this book, I am a wife, momma, and entrepreneur. I grew up in the small city of Thunder Bay, Ontario, with my parents and sister. My dad owned (and still owns) a business selling trailers, motorhomes, and boats, while my mom worked as an executive assistant for the school board and then Confederation College, where she was promoted to Director of Media Relations.

Growing up, we always had new houses, new cars, new downhill skis, new clothes, renovated houses, pools, and trips many times a year. As a kid, if you asked me, I'd say we were rich. Both my parents worked hard, and they enjoyed a specific lifestyle that was always showing our best selves outside the house. I grew up with an expectation that life looked a certain way, and that I was supposed to own a specific house, car and lifestyle.

Unfortunately, my happy childhood changed when I was in high school, and my parents divorced. My parents never argued in front of my sister or me, so it was a shock. But the bigger shock came during the years following, as our lifestyle drastically changed and everything we knew and expected fell apart around us. Within the year, my dad's business was bankrupt, our house was gone, our cars were changed, and my sister and I moved in with our Auntie Lynne and her two little children on the other side of town.

We likely didn't have as much hardship as others have experienced, but when your world is ripped out from under you, and everything you have known falls apart, your personal experience feels worse than anyone else's. I was fifteen when my parents' life was ripped apart, and it was my first experience to the financial woes of life.

I started working as a banquet waitress at a hotel and as a cashier at Burger King, and I began saving money. I have passionately worked ever since at every typical job; clothing stores, school campus jobs, waitress, bartender, and even made crafts to sell at local shows. I was taught to save, and I had my first bank account when I was ten, but no one ever taught me to budget and invest, so I have spent many years helping others figure out

Previous Healthcare

I have always had a passion for learning new things and challenging myself, so my first success in life was to move from Thunder Bay to Toronto for school. In 2002 I graduated from the Michener Institute of Applied Health Sciences as a Respiratory Therapist and successfully obtained a job at Mount Sinai Hospital. After 11 years in Toronto, I moved back to Thunder Bay and spent another ten years specializing in respiratory-related chronic diseases such as COPD and neuromuscular diseases. I loved being a respiratory therapist, and I loved getting to know my patients and their families, but I couldn't help thinking that all of them would pass away soon.

The hardest part of this career was during the last few years, while healthcare cuts for nursing occurred, followed by changes in managerial structures, the once enjoyable healthcare system became negative. Cultural negativity was prevalent, as so many people felt overworked and underappreciated. Within that same year, in a short period of time, I also lost a couple of patients who held a special place in my heart.

Through these years I bought, and sold a townhouse, a condo, two houses, got married and had two children, but even though I was in the throws of adult responsibilities, I was still struggling to make ends meet and living a paycheque-to-paycheque life.

Side Business to Make Extra Money

Even though I was earning an income in the $65,000-$80,000 range, I was still struggling to live the lifestyle that I assumed was normal. When I had my first son, I had just moved to Thunder Bay and bought my first house. Did I mention I was also a single parent? Well, I quickly realized that I needed more money than I had.

I became obsessed with budgeting and ways NOT to spend money. That obsession also included insisting on breastfeeding instead of formula because even though I believed it was best for my son, I was extremely fearful that I couldn't afford formula. My son was premature and wasn't breastfeeding well, so my fear increased every time he wouldn't latch properly, but one day my dad and his girlfriend showed up with a large amount of formula, and friends gave me bottles to use, and I realized then that I could figure out this obstacle and many others.

Once this weight was off my shoulders, I started thinking about ways to bring more money into the house. I started sewing, knitting, and crafting to sell, but there was a lot more time invested in than profits, so I started looking at other things. After a few months of research, I opened an online drop-shipping store selling organic and natural products. It was an incredible business opportunity that I could do from home with a few clicks of the computer, as well as benefit from some tax-saving strategies by having a home-based business.

I continued with this business for about five years and earned about $10,000-$15,000 each year. Some may think that isn't much, but as a very part-time side hustle with very little overhead, it was ideal in my life. When I met Patrick, now my husband, and we decided to have another child, life got busy, and I lost interest in my online business, so I closed the store.

I still worked in healthcare all those years, but the negative environment and getting close to patients and their families became very trying on my heart and my head. Eventually, I was burnt out and unable to function properly, so my doctor put me on medical leave. It took me eight months to get back to feeling myself again and to return to the hospital work. The hardest part was that even though I had changed, the negative environment did not change. If anything, it was worse, and I was able to recognize how quickly it affected my patients, the other healthcare workers, myself and especially my family. Within a few months of being back in the environment, I knew I needed to figure out which path best suited me.

Always Obsessed with Money

As much as anyone says that money does not make the world go around, I believe they are mistaken. Whether you are young, old, married, or single, in order to make it in this world, you need to have that desire to make your own money and be able to save properly, budget and invest. If you want the best life for yourself and your family, then you need to take steps to get yourself wanting to understand how money works and learn how to budget properly so that your future is a much brighter one! So many people eventually become lost if they have to do things on their own in regard to their money.

The best option for anyone is to meet with a financial professional at age 18 and review with them yearly or with any life changes. When I meet with clients, I help them make goals to invest and ensure their money so they can make their dreams a reality. It is good to become a little obsessed with money and to find a plan that works for you. There is no one template that fits every woman. We all have different *Shiny Things* we appreciate and need in life.

My personal must-haves are manicures, pedicures and dyed hair (I need to keep away the grey), but for others, it may be eating out, wine, Starbucks, shoes, purses, and other things. Now, don't get me wrong; money is not everything! There are most definitely other parts of your life that are considered more important than money, but it is important to be prepared no matter what. Do not wait until something happens to start protecting yourself financially.

Think about all those "what ifs" and what could happen to you in any situation. I am sure everyone you know has a story of money woes but take me as an example. I was not prepared for my first child, for the work-related burnout, nor for other things that came along, but though each of these, I had an obsessive mind for money and knew ways to get back on top. And now, I know that I can help others get the same benefits and see a much stronger financial future.

So, take a look for yourself, what would happen if you were not ready for the next distraction? Would you lose everything? Would you have enough money saved? These are things that most women do not think about, until it is too late. The best option for you is to think about all those "what ifs" and figure out how you could prevent them from happening. If you are always prepared, then you are less likely to have any financial burdens. This means, no matter what, that money does have a large importance when it comes to your life and what you want from it.

Never Say No to What I Want

I know I personally have made 'interesting' money-motivated decisions in my life, and no matter what anyone said, I could justify those decisions. I love travelling, and I have taken many trips because it just felt right, whether I had the money or not, but as I've grown in my financial mind and became obsessed with my money, I realized it is so much more fun to travel with money than travel on a small budget.

As women, we need to have our own lives, too, our own goals, and our own passions. You should never allow someone in your life, or even yourself, to give you a reason to say no to the things you want; if you want it, then make it happen! Honestly, I am 100% unable to say no to someone if they suggest going to a restaurant.

Here is my first dirty little secret obsession. I have a secret obsession for restaurants. I love food, looking at menus and tasting the food creations before I order. I am obsessed with the smells of different foods cooking, and I love the business and environment of all the people bustling around together. I am 100% obsessed with going out to eat, and even more obsessed with the idea if I get to sit on a patio. Because of this, I know that I need to include extra money into my restaurant budget, and that area is more flexible in my life.

My favourite part of being a financial professional is helping people obtain their dreams and goals, I truly believe you can have anything you want, and together we can find ways to work towards them. When I work with my clients, we first look at your personal dreams and goals; we will make a list to prioritize the next year, 5 years, 10 years and retirement, and then take steps to succeed, but always working in your dirty little secret obsessions.

When you are passionate about your dreams and goals then you will do whatever it takes to obtain them, nothing will get in the way. There may always be that little voice inside your head that tells you not to try something because you think you cannot make it happen. Instead of listening to that little voice, email me and I will help you to ignore it and encourage you. Tell yourself that you can succeed!

Why Am I Doing This?

I am doing this because I am just like so many others out there. My parents divorced, I've lost a loved one, I've suffered from work-related burnout, I've made interesting money-motivated decisions, and I've struggled with money, so why exactly did I decide to write this book? Well, simply put, there are so many women who coast through their paycheques, struggle to understand their financial situations, or are suddenly thrown into having to do their financial planning all on their own, and are left completely confused and lost. I would like every woman to have an understanding of how important it is to manage your money and know how to properly protect your future.

Why do this for you? Why make changes to your life? The real question is, why not? Why wouldn't you want to better your life and learn how to be financially stable all on your own? There is no perfect time to prepare yourself to become financially stable, but the longer you delay, the longer it will take to fully live your best life.

As a woman, I think it is incredibly important to know about my finances (how much I earn, how much debt I have, how to do my own taxes, how much money do I need to retire, etc.). Instead of being forced to find all that out when a problem in your life occurs, wouldn't you much rather have the knowledge ahead of time so you can prevent any problem from even coming to fruition?

There are always tasks that can be delayed, but why delay something that can give you a better, more stable life where you can feel financially independent and know you can take care of yourself no matter what happens? It is so common to ask, "Why do something when you do not know what the outcome could be?" But, is that a chance you'd be willing to take with your own future or your family's future? Imagine yourself living your life as you have been, and something unexpected happens. What happens then? Are you prepared? Or would you feel lost and not know which path to take next?

Drastic life changes can happen so quickly, so why not be prepared for them? Rather than not expecting any hardships, expect the unexpected and prepare yourself for any problem that may come your way. When you think ahead and come up with a plan for all those negative things that could happen, then if and when those issues do arise, they will not seem nearly as significant as they would if you had not planned ahead of time.

I'm sure you know someone who has or had cancer, heart attack, or a stroke. How did they and their family cope financially? Did they fully recover and return to work right away? Chances are they didn't expect to have this devastating illness occur, and they weren't prepared. Life is too short to spend the majority of it worrying about money when instead you could be enjoying it!

We as women finally have opportunities to have our money working for us, to save our own money, and build our own credit, so why not take advantage of that and together learn how to do it properly? Together, we will reach your dreams and goals while managing your financial distractions, so you aren't always chasing Butterflies and Shiny Things. Give yourself the future you know you deserve!

If you find any of the concepts confusing, please drop me an email at friendlyfinancecoach@gmail.com, and I would be happy to help.

MONEY ... LOVE IT OR HATE IT

Don't let your life be controlled by these three things:

Your Past, People, and Money

History of money

Money, as we know it now, has drastically changed over the years. Take a look back a couple of hundred years ago when bartering for personal goods was a way to obtain the things you wanted. Vegetable farmers would exchange potatoes with the baker for bread; butchers would exchange meat with the chicken farmers for eggs, and so on.

Those simplistic times no longer exist. The concept of "getting what you want" is age-old but essential to civilization, and the people who had more leverage in bartering were the people who had more wealth or a larger quantity of essentials.

If you look over the past hundred years, the cost of everything in our daily lives has increased substantially. In the 1920s, you could buy a house for around $10,000, which is crazy to even think about when researching the cost of a house now! Not only has the cost of homes increased but so has the cost of food, cars, daycare, etc. All of these have a high cost in the world we live in. You have to work hard to cover all your bills and still be able to save for your future. It's overwhelming, but it can be done.

Women have also seen many changes throughout history when it comes to money. In today's society, we have a lot more opportunities than women in past decades. We take it for granted that a woman is free to manage her finances, buy a car or a house, apply for a credit card, or invest as she would like, but it wasn't so long ago, in the 1970s when women were unable to obtain many of the luxuries we now experience.

Here is a brief historical timeline:

1880: A woman named Mary Gage opened a stock exchange for women who wanted to use their own money to speculate on railroad stocks. Check out the 1889 Wall Street Journal article about how "Female Speculators Rattle Wall Street Traditions."

1969: Colgate-Palmolive laid women off rather than letting them do physical labour. This was, of course, "to protect our ladies" and their delicate sensibilities (INSANITY). In *Bowe v Colgate-Palmolive,* an appeals court ruled physical labour cannot be limited to men.

1970: *Schultz v Wheaton Glass* came about after a company had a "brilliant" (read – not brilliant) way to get around that pesky equal pay act. Simply have a different job title for the same work! Men were "selector-packer-stackers," while women were the much different "selector-packers." Fortunately, a federal appeals court saw right through that one!

1972: Katharine Graham became the first woman to become CEO of a Fortune 500 company – the Washington Post.

1974: This year saw the passage of the *Equal Credit Opportunity Act*, which made it illegal to discriminate against someone based on their gender, race, religion, and national origin. So, for the first time, women were able to be issued a credit card in their name without their husband's signature.

1978: *The Pregnancy Discrimination Act* was passed, but before that, it was legal to fire a woman for being pregnant.

1981: Before this time, a husband could keep his spouse in the financial dark. Thanks to *Kirchberg v Feenstra*, where a man was told he didn't have the right to unilaterally take out a second mortgage on property held jointly with his wife. Do you know why he had to be told this? Because before this time, it was actually the law in Louisiana that you could do this.

1988: Believe it or not, this was when the *"Women's Business Ownership Act"* put an end to state laws requiring male co-signers. That's only thirty years ago!

2009: President Barack Obama signed the *Lilly Ledbetter Fair Pay Restoration Act*, which allows people to sue companies for pay discrimination even if more than six months have passed.

History of Money and Relationships

Until recently, men were the main breadwinners in a household, and women remained in the home instead of working and did not hold responsibilities such as budgeting, bill paying, or making large purchases. Men would go to work, and the women would stay home to do all the "womanly duties" like cleaning, cooking, and taking care of the children. But also, it used to be completely normal for girls to have lived with their parents until they got married and moved in with their husbands. Women never had to worry about the financial aspects of life because the men always took care of that. It was deemed as "normal" for wives to trust that there was enough money for everything; no questions asked, it was just accepted. So, girls have learned that while growing up, they didn't have to talk about money.

My goal in life is to help girls/women of all ages understand that talking about money is a good thing. As women, we have gained so many more rights over the years, and we should take full advantage of that! Females of all ages should know how to handle their own finances and build their own credit. In the end, it benefits you! Let's open ourselves up to the universe to love our relationship with money and all the amazing things it offers us!

For many centuries, marriage was a financial transaction. Normally, the husband and wife had never met, or at least barely knew each other, and the woman was just expected to move away with a complete stranger and trust that he would be able to take care of her. And then, in the modern era, when marriage became about falling in love and free love, and finding your soul mate, people were looking for true love without asking some of the most important questions, which is what drives a long-term partnership.

I think having similar financial values is crucial. An abundance of marriages are destroyed because husbands and wives do not share the same financial values or dreams. It does not matter if you are a profligate spender or an industrious saver. You both have to be on the same page. If one person loves to save and have great credit, and the person they are married to just spends and spends, then how is that marriage supposed to work?   Lengthy battles over money will not only cause constant stress and problems within your marriage but can also cause it to break down. Of course, couples are going to have their difficulties, but it is important to treat each other as equals and have the same opinions about finances. Find a way to properly communicate your opinions and worries about money, so it is all out in the open. That way, your time is spent more productively, enjoying life with your family rather than having added tension.

Money and Romance

Why is it that money is such a nerve-wracking topic to discuss when in a new romance? For so many people, this subject seems so taboo! I think it is because, for a lot of people, our sense of self-worth and our self-esteem are wrapped up in our financial situation. And many people are scared to discuss it out of fear of being judged by the person that they are romantically involved with.

The tradition of not talking about money and not talking about your salary is something that has been long-standing over the past 40 years. I think that it's private because people don't want to reveal that personal part of themselves. If someone does not make as much as the other person, they may be nervous that the person they're involved with may no longer be interested. But that is the issue! People are so worried about the other person's reaction that finances are never discussed, and that is where the problem begins.

For a lot of people, it's all wrapped up in how successful they are as a person. Money, and stress over finances, are very powerful forces in intimate relationships because whether you have a lot of money or a little money, the topic is always there. You don't ever escape its power. But there are ways to work with your partner so that money does not take over the relationship. Wives come to me to straighten out finances before their husbands find out.

Equality of Men and Women in the Workplace

The topic of equality of men and women in the workplace has been an endless debate that is still going on to this day. Women have needed to constantly prove they are equals in a world full of men. Why is it that women need to debate with powerful people that they deserve the same rights as men?

We work so hard for our families and even ourselves. We take education just as seriously as men, but yet we are deemed the lower half compared to men. This has slowly started to change, but there is still a long way to go until women of all demographics feel comfortable and secure in the workplace. In a lot of workplaces, women have to work twice as hard to have their efforts noticed. Women are just as capable, yet the world still makes us feel like we are less than the powerful, rich man who doesn't consider us any more than a housewife. Now, this is not everyone, but there are still people in our society who do not believe women deserve the same rights, and that is something we are constantly trying to fight against and prove untrue.

There are obviously some positive changes that have given women the opportunity to explore any career their heart's desire. There used to be a time when the only careers "suited" for women were nurses and secretaries, so it is clear we have come a long way. Now we can go to school for practically anything we are interested in. We have the option to apply for the career we want, and we can follow any path we are interested in to find the perfect fit for us.

To top it all off, we can feel confident that we will actually be heard and listened to, whereas one hundred years ago, we couldn't even imagine that being possible. We can now walk into a workplace and make our voices and opinions heard, and, in most workplaces, we do not feel judged in any way. Women have come so far in a really short time, and that should be noticed and applauded!

Women's Needs Cost More

When you look at the costs of products for women, you wouldn't automatically assume that they would be higher than the costs for a similar product made for men. This may be something that both men and women really do not think about, but it is factual! Deodorant, clothing, vehicles, and so much more, cost women extra money, and not many people choose to question this.

Not only do women pay extra for the same products that men have, but we also have to spend money on things that men do not need to. Feminine products are a necessity for most women, and we just automatically tailor that into our costs, without realizing it is just the female side of our society who have that cost. There are also costs for children. It is usually assumed that the woman in the relationship takes care of the costs for the child or children. Not that we are complaining about buying cute things for our kids, but all of these have an extra cost that does add up at the end of the month.

There was a study done in the *Journal of Real Estate, Finances, and Economics* that stated that women receive higher rates for mortgages. The reason for this is that women normally end up going to a bank or institution from a recommendation, whereas men do their research and find the best rate possible. I believe the main reason for this is because mortgages are a fairly new concept for women. It used to be the men who would deal with the finances, and women would just trust it was all getting done the right way.

Money and Stress

Money and stress; what a terrible combination! Stressing over money can really take a toll on your daily life. Not only do you probably think about money daily, but you also have so many different ways of spending your money or even seeing how much money is in your bank account.

In today's society, money is one of the things that is always on our minds. This can be a great thing if you have a constant inflow of money, but if you're on the other end of the spectrum where you have bills left unpaid, or other debts, then you are constantly reminded of those issues, and that can add so much stress on your life. If you have a phone, or even the internet, you will hear about any unpaid bill pretty quickly. Sometimes it can feel like, no matter how much you try to live your life, your money problems are always in the spotlight.

My clients tell me that not only can financial issues cause you to have money always on the brain, but they can also cause some health issues. Being constantly surrounded by the new product, the new big thing, and having to see others living a much more luxurious life than you can really affect how you live your daily life.

How Does Money Form Our Decisions?

Money is success, failure, control, submission, love and hate. Money can mean the chance at motherhood or the end of a marriage. When you truly look at it, money is everything and nothing, all at the same time. It forms most of the decisions we make in our lives. Looking at the big picture of currency in general, it really is only just pieces of paper (or plastic depending on where you are located). But yet we are always concerned over it and strive to make as much of it as possible.

Society has made us all want to make every decision based around money, and that has made both positive and negative changes. People are more concerned with how much money they have compared to the person standing next to them than they are sometimes with actually enjoying life! There has to be that balance.

Whether it comes to starting school, getting married, having children, every choice we make goes back to how much money we have in our pocket. If you have money problems or any debt, that is usually something that is always in the back of your mind. How will I pay it off? When will I be out of debt? These are all questions most people ask themselves at least once in their lives.

Money can end up taking over your life if you constantly fixate on it. Every day you come home to see a new bill in your mailbox, it brings you down and can make you feel like you will never get out of that dark pit we call debt. It can make you feel all alone in a world full of people enjoying their life and the money they saved. For something that isn't even a living being, it can really take a toll on your mind, body, and soul.

Is Your Money Sabotaging you?

Is money starting to become an issue for you? Are you so wrapped up in it that you can no longer see the clear picture? There is such a thing as having your life too wrapped up around your money. If that is all you think about, it will completely take over! Life is too short to worry constantly over something that can be a stress-free part of your life.

There is another way money can sabotage you. What if you spend more money than you have? If you do not have a budget set in place for yourself, it will be rather difficult to keep track of your spending and what you are spending all your cash on. This can not only put you in debt, but also cause you long-term stress, which can eventually affect your health.

Your mindset, such as ambivalence about money, love for money, or anger about money, has a large impact on how money can affect you. This is why making a plan and having a budget are so important, as well as changing your mindset can bring more joy into your life. Ultimately, if you are overspending and avoiding your bills, then you are only sabotaging yourself. I help women like you to organize and change their mindsets and love how much money you have so you no longer feel "sabotaged" by your money!

How do you Suppose the Recession will Affect Women's Thinking About Money?

Personally, I think it's going to have an enormous impact and what's going on now is so serious, yet it hasn't even remotely begun to play out. I think that without a second Depression, these issues are powerful and can really transform people's relationships. But I think now, when people's lifestyles and very careers are being threatened, all of these things are going to be in the forefront and wield an even stronger influence.

If you're not careful and on track with your finances, your whole way of life could have a dramatic impact.

Even if there isn't a global recession, so many people are losing the jobs that they thought were secure and needed to maintain their household bills, feed their families and themselves, as well as plan for their retirement.

With inflation rates, everything keeps costing more, but people are not getting paid enough to cover all their expenses. I believe women should always be on their toes when it comes to money; always be ahead of the game. Obviously, there are certain circumstances that you will not be able to take into consideration, but when it comes to the recession, there are steps you can take to avoid major losses and struggles.

What do Women Want?

What exactly do women want? I believe women want a variety of different things in life; happiness, love, independence, trust, and security. And, what do women want in terms of finances? Women want similar things in relationships as they want in terms of finances; security, understanding and independence are the top needs.

The first step is to get education on budgeting, saving, and future financial planning. To feel confident in your financial future, women need to have education about it first. Women want help in managing household finances quickly and easily. The most common stressor is managing household finances, and having that dealt with always leads to calm, and emotional stability. They also want proper financial advice that is geared to their specific goals and dreams. Every person is different, so you cannot follow simple guidelines that are geared towards everyone!

Surprisingly, only 11 percent of women prefer to work with a female financial advisor; the majority (85 percent) said that they were indifferent to the gender of their banker. But in my experience, more women in finance can only be a good thing. Several studies show that women take more risks and achieve more consistent and higher gains on funds they manage. Women should want someone who can personally understand all the costs that they have and how to succeed even with those costs. As qualified as a male financial advisor may be, a female advisor can better understand the wants and needs of a woman, and make a plan that fits perfectly for your lifestyle!

I think the idea of women dealing with their own finances is still so new that women are reluctant to even attempt doing it because they are afraid of failing. There are so many options for women now, and we really should do our research and find what fits best for our lives.

Homework:

1) What is Your Money Personality Type?

https://www.investopedia.com/articles/basics/07/money-personality.asp

Are you a Big Spender, Saver, Shopper, Debtor, or Investor? Check out this article to understand what type of money personality type you are.

2) What thoughts, feelings, emotions did your parents have about money? What are your thoughts, feelings, emotions surrounding money?

3) Write down your belief and emotions about money. Are there statements you recognize you continuously say? It's time to stop saying, "I don't have enough money to "…." and replace it with "Won't it be exciting when I can "……"! How can you change the statements you say to yourself?

JENNIFER WOODBECK

WHAT IS A FINANCIAL NEEDS ANALYSIS?

Your net worth to the world is usually determined by what remains after your bad habits are subtracted from your good ones.

- Benjamin Franklin, founding father of the USA

Dreams and Goals

The very first step in any financial needs analysis is stating your dreams and goals. When we are kids, we dream of doing many things; having a special house or car, trips around the world, or relaxing in our favourite space without any need to go somewhere. We have all these dreams at some point in our lives, but being young, we do not have a clue about what they cost.

As we get older, we stop dreaming or at least starting believing that our dreams are out of reach for financial reasons. Once we begin to learn how expensive things are, we start worrying that all we have dreamt of is out of reach. Well, I am here to help you dream again!

As a teenager, I was told to dream big and marry rich. When I would say, "Look at that car! I want a car like that when I grow up," the response was usually, "Well, you better marry rich." But marrying rich is not the only way of getting what you want in your life. Now you have the option of making your own dreams come true!

What I've been able to do over the years is help women and men, figure out their dreams and goals, and actually make them come true. Is your dream to buy a new car, buy a new house, take a vacation, retire at a specific age, or just to work less? Every person has an image of how they want their lives to be. No matter what your dreams and goals are, do you have a plan to get there, or do you plan to live off credit?

I believe that if you want to be successful, and have all your dreams come true, then you have to take the right steps and stick to a plan. Getting <u>all</u> you want in your life is never an easy process, but it is definitely rewarding! The first step in a financial needs analysis is to plan your dreams and goals, then look at how to get there without using credit.

What are your top 3 dreams and goals?

- o Buy a new car
- o Buy a new home
- o Buy a cottage
- o Take a vacation
- o Retire at age _____
- o Work less
- o Make more money
- o Save for children's education
- o Pay off mortgage early

- o Pay off bad debt
- o Protect income in case of loss
- o Have an emergency fund
- o Have a game plan for retirement
- o Ensure proper insurance protection
- o Leave an estate for your family

When you look at the list of dreams and goals, the majority of them cost money or may cost you more money now and less money down the road. Consider that, and then answer this question. Can your dreams and goals be met by your current income? If your answer to that question is no, then what needs to change?

What do you need to do differently to reach your dreams and goals? What kind of timeline are you looking at for reaching your goals? Getting what you want from life is never an easy task, but it is the most rewarding in the end. Having a plan set in place to reach your goals is the best way to actually succeed.

If you just tell yourself, "It will happen," is that going to fix anything, or are you going to be in the same situation of wanting but not having it actually change? If you really want to succeed at achieving your dreams and goals, then put in the effort! This is not something that can be done overnight but is definitely worth it when all is said and done.

Assets vs Debts (Liabilities)

If you are not familiar with any financial terms, then the words "Assets and Debts" may be quite confusing. These terms can also add a lot of stress in your life because debt is normally a word that we tend to look at negatively. Well, ladies, I am here to tell you it is not that complicated!

Essentially, liability and debt are one and the same so when discussing assets and debt, what we are looking at is how much you are actually worth. Also known as your Net Worth. This is done by looking at what you have in a bank plus what you have your money invested in, compared to what you owe, or in other words, your debt.

Your assets could include a home, cottage, condo, your vehicle, and any investments such as RRSP, TFSA, pension, RESP, GIC, LIRA, savings accounts, and emergency funds. Your assets are beneficial to you. They are what you bring in when it comes to money (bank accounts), as well as what you have (materialistic items) that have already been purchased. All these assets give you a total of what you are worth. This number obviously changes though, when you take a look at your liabilities.

Your liabilities are what you owe or have to pay back and could include credit card balances, loans, line of credit, and mortgage. This money would come from your assets, and hopefully, by the end, you still have a positive number! If not, then taking a look at your budget and costs may be a good way to see why you are spending more than you actually have. More information about this is available in Chapter 5.

Assets- Debts= Net Worth

It is important to keep track of all your finances, especially all that you owe. If you have more than one credit card, remember to keep track and know exactly how much you owe each one, so you do not get behind. Both assets and liabilities are grouped together. So, it does not matter if you are fully paying off one liability; if you miss a payment on one, it affects your credit as a whole. If you have a good handle on your money, then you should have more assets than liabilities. This means you have enough money to cover all your costs so you can avoid going into further debt.

Financial Independence Number

I am sure many of you have not heard of your "Financial Independence Number," or if you have heard of it before, you may be unsure of what it is. Well I am here to tell you! The Financial Independence Number is whatever amount of money you would need to live off without any other inflow of money. Many people look at the Financial Independence Number as the retirement plan number. What is your magic number so that you would not need to work ever again, yet you could pay your bills for the rest of your life and feel truly comfortable? This number is really important and should be figured out early so you can plan. There is a financial independence number for everyone. It's just a matter of figuring out what it is!

When it comes to finding out your Financial Independence Number, there are some steps to follow. An excellent way to start is to look at how much money you think you would need monthly to live comfortably. So, look at what you spend monthly now, as that will give you a great estimate. This will need to include all your monthly costs; housing, clothing, food, bills, debt, etc.

Your next step would be simply multiplying your monthly amount by 12 (12 months in a year), and that will give you an idea of how much money you will be required to have yearly. One thing you want to take into account is that inflation does happen. For example, a loaf of bread in 1990 cost $1.37, but today it costs $2.67. The average inflation rate is 3.13%, so as certain costs will go up, it would be a good idea to assume the average inflation rate and have a little extra monthly just in case.

Now what you will have to do is take a look at your safe withdrawal rate. A safe withdrawal rate is a certain amount that you can take out of your total net worth each year without having a fear of running out of your money before you pass away. A common percentage that is used is a withdrawal rate is 4%. This is due to a study done in 1998 (The Trinity Study) that states that a 4% withdrawal rate will make it, so it is rather difficult for you to ever run out of money, if you are not overspending, of course. However, this study is a little outdated, but it is still recommended to use a 3-4% withdrawal rate.

The last step is a simple equation that will give you your financial independence number. This equation is "Yearly Spending" divided by your "Withdrawal Rate." The total you get will be that magic number that is your Financial Independence Number. Once you know your number, you can take a look at the steps you would need to make in your life to become completely financially independent!

Example

Let's assume you are 30 years old and want to retire at age 60. To cover all your expenses and allow extra you require $3000 per month.

$3000x12=$36,000 yearly

Let's assume the inflation rate is 3%, we need to know how much money in 30 years will be equal $36,000 today.

Amount=Principle (1+interest rate/1)$^{1(number\ of\ years)}$

A=36000(1+.03/1)$^{1(30)}$

Amount = $87381.45

So, $36,000 today will be $87,381.45 in 30 years.

The last step is to calculate the yearly spending by the withdrawal rate of 4%.

$87381.45/ .04= $2,184,536.22 is needed to retire at age 60.

For this example of someone 30 years old planning to retire at 60 years old with equivalent to $36,000 a year their Financial Independence Number is $2,184,536.

True Costs of Credit

The idea of credit and having a credit card has been around since roughly the 1920s. This means that most people today do not know of a life without credit. Credit is something people automatically use, but what if credit no longer existed? A lot of people in our society would have an issue with that, as it is mostly what they live off. Having some form of credit can be considered both a positive and negative thing.

I would look at credit as a positive contribution to people's lives because of the fact that you can purchase things you wouldn't normally be able to purchase if you were just using your monthly income. Big purchases would take so much longer to save for, and ultimately, it could make your life a lot more complicated. But there are also some negative sides I see to having credit cards and purchasing things on credit.

A negative aspect is that people can put themselves deep into debt if they are not tracking their spending. If you make a certain amount of money, banks notice that and tend to offer you credit cards just because they can! As wonderful as this sounds, if you cannot pay off your monthly fees to those credit cards, then you are creating a big problem for yourself. If you are just paying the minimum on your monthly fees for anything you've paid for with credit, then you are causing a never-ending spiral that will just put you further into debt. If you are not paying off those cards in full, then you are accumulating interest. This means paying the minimum really will not make a difference as your interest rate will keep climbing and increasing the amount of money you owe.

There are some tips I would recommend to avoid allowing your credit to get out of control. Try to stick to one or two credit cards. Too many can get far too overwhelming, which can cause you to miss payments. There is no reason to have an abundance of credit cards.

If you deal with just one or two, you can build up your credit and actually get better interest rates if you continuously pay off those cards when you're supposed to. If you have more than two cards, do not panic; just work to close those accounts. Too many credit cards can negatively affect your credit, so just make sure to keep up with all your monthly payments and keep track of each card.

Another recommendation would be to take a look at different credit card companies. Many people do not think about it, but different companies offer different interest rates. You want to look for the company with the best interest rates and the best options for you. Not only do the rates vary, but there are certain cards that can really benefit you! There are so many different options for you that you can find a card that is personalized towards your own lifestyle.

Watch for fees within a credit card. Some credit companies provide points or rewards, but you may pay fees for those cards. Credit card companies may offer you loan protection, credit protection insurance, disability insurance or life insurance within their credit card. This type of insurance will pay the credit card company if something happened to you, but this may not be needed if you have proper personal insurance, which would pay your beneficiary instead of the banks. More information regarding this can be found in Chapter 4.

Credit is not a word to be scared of, but it is something to keep on top of, or it can get out of hand. There are some circumstances where you should veer away from using credit, but building your credit can give you so many more options as far as making large purchases and being able to do what you want in life. My advice is to build positive credit, and that is done by keeping track of your finances and avoid missing any payments.

Rule of 72

The rule of 72 is a concept that you may have been taught in high school, but possibly do not remember. The rule of 72 was made famous by Albert Einstein but was not actually invented by him. It was said to originate from a man named Luca Pacioli, dates back to around 1494 AD, and was found in a book titled *"Summa De Arithmetica."* This is just an estimate though, as some people believe the rule of 72 has been around even longer.

The rule of 72 is a mathematical concept that approximates the number of years it takes to double your money based on your interest rate. When your money is invested at a bank, the current average interest rate is less than 1%. So, as an example, let's use 1% for easy math. If you invest $10,000 at the age of 29 with a 1% interest rate, it will take you 72 years for your money to double. Therefore, your $10,000 that was invested at the age of 29 will now double to be $20,000 at the age of 108! Well, I don't know about you, but I do not want to wait that long for my money to double. Personally, I would like a faster solution that gives me what I want in life.

Now let's start getting your money working harder for you!

I have successfully been able to help people with a 6% interest rate. So, let's take a look at those numbers again! If we take that same $10,000 at the age of 29, and invested at 6%, your money doubles every 12 years. At the age of 41, your money is now $20,000, at the age of 53, your money is $40,000. At the age of 65, which is around the average age of retirement, your investment is going to be at about $80,000.

Even better, if you take a look at an interest rate of 12% at the age of 65; that amount of $10,000 you invested at the age of 29 is now at $640,000, so your money has the potential to double every 6 years. Now let's think about this! What does the average interest rate on a credit card or a loan cost? At the time of writing this book, the average credit card interest rate is between 20% to 24%. If you have a credit card at the age of 29 with a balance of $10,000, then you could owe as much as $20,000 before the age of 33, if you are not on top of paying it off every month.

These are some of the most important concepts to understand as you begin your journey towards reaching your financial dreams and goals.

Homework:

1) List your top 3 dreams and goals

2) Figure out your Net Worth (Assets-Debts=Net Worth)

3) Figure out your Financial Independence Number

JENNIFER WOODBECK

FUN AND CRAZY ACRONYMS

Being financially educated is a necessity not a luxury

Have you ever looked at financial terms and thought to yourself, "How am I ever going to understand all this?!" You are not alone! Some people do not bother doing their research on what it all means because it seems like a lot of effort for something you can get someone else to do for you. I believe it is important to "know your stuff" when it comes to finance. so that when you decide to make a financial plan, you know exactly what you are talking about!

TFSA

A TFSA is a Tax-Free Savings Account that is used in Canada for anyone over the age of 18 to get tax free growth for the money they save. This type of savings plan started in 2009 to help individuals save money without paying as much income tax. Almost any bank, investment company or insurance company will offer some kind of a tax-free savings account, and they all follow the same guidelines as this is a savings account that was created by the government and is used through CRA. Since 2009 the TFSA contribution room continues to increase, and if you have never contributed to a TFSA, you are able to contribute for all the previous years, after the age of 18.

Here are the amounts for previous years since the inception of the TFSA:

2009- $5000

2010-$5000

2011-$5000

2012-$5000

2013-$5500

2014-$5500

2015-$10,000

2016-$5500

2017-$5500

2018-$5500

2019-$6000

2020-$6000

So, if you have never contributed to a TFSA and you were older than 18 years old in 2009, you can invest $63,500 into a TFSA.

If you are unsure of your contribution room, you can check the Canadian Revenue Agency (CRA) website in your CRA account or call them. But be aware that the CRA website is updated at the end of each year. It is simple to set up a tax-free savings account, all you need is your SIN and your date of birth. Keep in mind that even though they are called a 'savings' account, in order to get the best investment growth it is best to think of it as a 'tax-free investment account' with the intention to leave the money in the account for long term growth.

RRSP

An RRSP, or a Registered Retirement Savings Plan as some people may know it, is a great tool to use to invest your money in your future retirement plan. This particular savings plan was created in 1957 and is currently connected with the Canada Revenue Agency (CRA), so everything is done legally and to fully benefit you. This can be used for both those employed by businesses and self-employed individuals.

There are quite a few different types of RRSPs. One is an Individual RRSP, which can only be used by one person and can only have their money/earnings contributed. Another form of RRSP is one for spouses, which is most obviously called the Spousal RRSP. This type of RRSP can have two people (who are within a marriage) contribute their earnings, or can also have one person contribute their money, and then that money would be divided equally between both parties.

A Group RRSP is one that is normally set up by your workplace. Your workplace may not necessarily have this, but if they do, you would have the option to take money out of your income and put it into this Group RRSP. Another type of RRSP that is similar to the Group RRSP is a Pooled RRSP. The only major difference between the two is that a Group RRSP is normally used for larger companies, whereas a Pooled RRSP is normally used with smaller businesses or even self-employed individuals.

There are a few benefits of an RRSP. One benefit is that what you contribute in a year can be used as a deduction on your tax return. For example, in Ontario, if you are in the top tax bracket, for every $1000 you contribute, you can reduce your income tax payment by approximately $535. If you aren't in the top tax bracket, there are still financial tax-saving benefits, but they will vary from the example above.

A second benefit to an RRSP is that you can carry forward your contribution to future years so you may have tax benefits when you need them. A third benefit is that your investment earnings are tax-free, as long as they stay in your RRSP, so it allows the tax-free compounding to grow faster. A fourth benefit is that you can transfer the RRSP tax-free into an RRIF or Annuity, an explanation of both can be found later on in this chapter, but the benefits for each are that you will only pay tax on the payments you receive each year, so if you're in a lower tax bracket in retirement, you'll pay less tax.

A final benefit is that unlike other forms of savings plans, an RRSP has the option of withdrawal at any time, even before planned retirement, but you will pay taxes. The amount of taxes paid will depend on the amount you withdraw; $1-$4,999 you will pay 10% tax, $5,000-$15,000, you will pay 20% tax, and any amount over $15,000, you will pay 30% tax (everywhere in Canada except Quebec).

Keep in mind that an RRSP withdrawal will be added onto your yearly income amount so your total taxable income will increase, and therefore the amount of income tax you pay at the end of the year may also increase. In addition to your income tax, some companies may have additional specific conditions, so make sure to do your research prior to making any decisions.

It is not recommended to withdraw your money prior to retirement because of the huge risk of not having enough money to cover your lifestyle before you pass. For example, if you withdraw $6000 from your RRSP now, after 25 years (assuming your interest rate is 7% yearly), your RRSP will have over $32,000 less in it.

RRIF

RRIF, also known as Registered Retirement Income Fund, is one of the most flexible and tax-effective ways to generate a retirement income. An RRIF is an account that is registered with the federal government that provides you with an income in your retirement years. You can open an RRIF by transferring money from your

RRSP, but it must be done no later than the end of the year you turn 71.

A benefit of an RRIF is that any money left in it when you die will go to your beneficiary or your estate. One of the disadvantages of an RRIF is that there is a minimal amount that must be withdrawn on a yearly basis and it increases as you get older, so it may not benefit your tax-saving strategies in retirement.

LIRA

LIRA stands for "Locked in Retirement Account," and it is another type of pension plan that is in Canada and helps you properly save for your retirement. Just like the name states, this account set up for retirement is locked until you officially retire, so there is no way you can have those funds released until you are no longer working.

This type of account is made to hold money from various pension plans, whether it is from a previous workplace or from a spouse who has passed away. This guarantees your money is being held and protected so that you can make sure you will have enough funds to cover yourself once retired.

As stated, these funds are held up until retirement; however, you do have the opportunity to move the funds to another account if deemed necessary. This can be for a variety of reasons, including if you happen to switch banking institutions and need to transfer your money to another retirement savings account.

While in the majority of situations, your funds are locked until retirement, there are a few reasons in which you may have to get your money released earlier than retirement. One reason to be able to access funds early will be if your income is so low that you are unable to cover your costs. This would include if you are at risk of losing your home as well. This obviously varies based on your situation, but there is a chance you could access the money earlier, depending on your circumstances.

Another reason you may be able to access your LIRA early is if your life expectancy has shortened, and you may not make it to retirement age. In those circumstances, funds would be reassessed, and you could have your money released prior to actually retiring. Setting up a LIRA account is a great way to guarantee you will have enough money to cover you and your family once you do retire.

Many other retirement savings accounts give you more lenient options for accessing the money early, whereas with a LIRA account, your options are more limited, and you will normally have to wait until you have officially retired to access your money.

Reference: https://www.investopedia.com/terms/l/locked-in-retirement-account.asp

RESP

An RESP, or a Registered Education Savings Plan, is a great way to save and grow money tax-free for your children's future and invest in their education. There is no tax on the investment earnings as long as they stay in the plan. This Canadian savings plan gives parents or caregivers an opportunity to put a certain amount of their income away so that when their kids finish high school, there is money saved to put them through college or university without a heavy burden of financial stress.

Just like a lot of savings plans that are connected through the CRA, the government will make contributions to the RESP, so as you continue to invest your money, you are also getting tax-free money placed into the account to help you and your family out that much more! You can put up to a maximal of $50,000 per child into the investment. Lower-income families may open an RESP without personal contributions and may qualify for additional Canada Learning Bond contributions. If you live in Quebec, Alberta or Saskatchewan, there are additional grants you may be eligible for.

If the child decides to delay post-secondary education after high school, they can still use an RESP up to 36 years of age (in some specific plans, they can be opened up to 40 years). So how does an RESP work once a child ventures into their next level of education? Once the person is enrolled in their school program, they can actually start using the money that you invested. An additional benefit is that the withdrawals are considered as the student's income, and likely they won't have much income so they won't have to pay much income tax also.

One concern I hear most often is, "What if my child doesn't go to school?" or "What if they drop out or don't use all the money?". Well, some of the great advantages of the RESP is that it can stay open until age 36, so if the child doesn't go to school right away, they may change their mind later. Or another option I provide is to open a family plan so the money can be used between all siblings included in the plan. And the third option is to transfer up to $50,000 tax-free from the RESP to a RRSP as long as a few qualifications are met.

Investment Terms (Stocks, Shares, Bonds, GIC, MF, ETF, and Segregated Funds)

An investment is something that you put money into that can help with your future and give you more money than you originally invested. This can include something you do individually, or you can pool your money together with a larger group of investors. In Canada, there are quite a few different types of investments, depending on what you are looking for.

Stocks, Shares, and Bonds

Investing in stock can seem like a scary venture, but many people look to investing in stocks as a way to make extra money. In simple terms, investing in the stock of a certain company or business means you are putting money into the said company in return for a small percentage of ownership. This means you are eligible to receive a portion of the company's earnings, usually through dividends (payouts) or some other form of payment.

A company normally sells stock to the public so they can properly operate their businesses and be able to cover all their costs. As said above, if you invest in stock with a company, you are paying to have some ownership with the company. Usually, it is a good option to invest with larger businesses that have a high standing but be aware, you will be paying higher than with other companies. You could invest with smaller and lesser-known businesses, but then you are more at risk of losing your money because you are unaware of how the company could do in the next couple of years. You need a good understanding of the stability of a company.

Depending on how much stock you invest in, you will have a certain number of shares considered your percentage of ownership with the company. For example, if you invested in a company and have 500 shares and the company has 500,000 shares in total, then you would have 1% ownership of the company, so you would be entitled to 1% of that business's earnings.

A bond is a loan or money owed to either a financial institution, business, or the government. The bond would have details about the loan, whose name the loan is in, and how much is owed. It will also include the end date for the bond, which is when you would have to make sure that the loan is covered in full, as well as any interest that may have accumulated.

GIC

One of the types of investments most people have heard of is a GIC (Guaranteed Investment Certificate). A GIC works like a deposit where you agree to lend the bank your money for a set number of months or years (term). The most common terms are 6 months, 1 year, 2 years or up to 10 years, and typically the longer the term, the higher the interest rate.

This is one of the more popular investments because the money that you lend is protected, as well as the interest that you receive while having your GIC. As long as the GIC has an end date no later than five years, and has an amount less than $100,000, your money will remain protected.

The best thing about GICs is that normally there are no fees to buy a GIC. But there may be a penalty if you break the contract term in order to get your money back earlier than the end date on the GIC.

GICs are considered a low-risk investment because you are guaranteed to get whatever you initially invested, but there are still some risks. The first risk is that the interest rate you are guaranteed is often not as high as the rate of inflation, so that means the growth on your GIC is low. A second risk occurs when a GIC is invested with variable returns because the interest rate isn't fixed, so it's based on the performance of things like the stock market. If the market does well, so does your interest rate, but if the market doesn't do well, your interest rate could be nothing at all. This also means you aren't keeping up with the rate of inflation.

Mutual Funds

Another form of investment is an MF, or in other words, a Mutual Fund. Mutual funds normally have numerous different types of investments (stocks, bonds and other types of security), and as an investor, you personally have no say in what it is invested in. Because a mutual fund is a pooled investment, you're putting your money into the group, and a portfolio manager will buy shares of the fund. This can leave you with a lot of questions because you do not really have a choice in what types of securities this mutual fund is investing in.

Mutual fund portfolios will be diversified, which means your investment is shared amongst many stocks and bonds. This is a positive for mutual fund investing because when you are invested in numerous companies or stocks and one decreases in worth, it does not affect your mutual fund portfolio as much as other investments that have all your money invested in one place. One of the disadvantages of mutual funds is that the level of risk and return is based solely on what the funds are invested in.

Mutual Funds are not guaranteed or insured so you may not get back the money you initially invested. It is beneficial to understand the past performance of a fund but acknowledge that the past performance does not determine how it will perform in the future. Another disadvantage is that mutual funds have fees that reduce your investment return.

ETF

An ETF, or known as an exchange-traded fund, is similar in some ways to a mutual fund. An ETF invests in stocks and bonds owned by a pooled group of people and has professional money managers, similar to a mutual fund. The biggest difference is that ETFs are traded on the stock exchange and are sold or exchanged quickly. You typically pay fees such as commissions to someone to invest in ETFs, and there may be costs to set up the investment account. The level of risk and return will depend on the ETF investments so you can lose money investing in ETFs.

Segregated Funds

Segregated funds are an option for investing that are sold by life insurance companies. Unlike mutual funds, segregated funds come with insurance guarantees because essentially, they are individual insurance contracts. These funds come with guarantees such as protecting part of the money you invest, anywhere from 75%-100% of your investment.

An advantage to segregated funds is that even if the funds you are invested in lose money, you are guaranteed to get back some or all of your principal investment. But keep in mind that your contract will state the number of years needed to invest before you can benefit from the guarantee. Another advantage of this type of investment is that it provides potential creditor protection, which most funds do not. And one of my favourite features of the segregated fund is the guaranteed death benefit. This means that depending on your contact type (75%-100%), your beneficiaries will receive your contributions tax-free when you die and will avoid probate fees.

Some of the disadvantages to segregated funds are that you need to keep your money in the fund until the maturity date to get the guarantees, and there may be penalties for early withdrawals. Another disadvantage is that this type of fund also has MER, just like mutual funds do.

MER

MER, or Management Expense Ratio, is a fee that calculates all the costs that were made to keep certain investments going. These fees are turned into a percentage which may affect the return you get. This calculation is normally done annually and gives you the best idea of how much money it takes to keep investments running smoothly.

This calculation is done by dividing the total amount of the investment's costs by the total amount of the investment's assets. Expenses or costs of the investment vary depending on what you use the said investment for, and how much it takes to keep the investment operating or running properly. Certain costs could include taxes or legal services, but it really depends based on what type of investment you have set up.

An MER is important, especially for investors, because they look at this calculation to see if it is a worthy investment to put their money into.

Annuity

An Annuity is like a paycheque. Annuities provide a set payment plan for you similar in concept to an income, but a disadvantage is that they do not always keep up with inflation. An annuity is taxed as income and will provide some income for life but remember that payments will end when you die.

Dividends

Dividends are a portion of a company's net earnings that are paid out to the shareholders, or to anyone that owns or has invested in that company's stock. This is pretty much your gift for investing in the company. A large amount of a company's earnings is not used towards dividends, but instead is used to keep the business in good standing financially, and then the remainder is given out to shareholders.

Dividends are paid out either quarterly or annually, based on the structure. There are also different ways in which dividends can be given. Some companies issue their dividends through cash, deposit, or stocks; it all depends. That being said, not all companies pay dividends.

Some companies will still pay out dividends even if the business is not in high standing financially, so that is definitely something to look out for! If you are looking into investing in a company and receiving dividends, look at larger, well-known companies. An example of this would be oil and gas businesses, or banks and financial institutions.

Another thing to keep an eye on is the dates for dividends payments. There is something called an ex-dividend date, and this is simply the date that you will no longer be able to invest in stock to receive a dividend. Another date to glance at is a record date, and that is when the company will make final decisions on which shareholders will be receiving dividends. The last date would be the payment date, and this would be when you receive your share!

<u>Leverage</u>

Leverage, in the financial aspect of it, is when you borrow shares in a stock from a broker in the hope of increasing your profit. If you borrow shares at $1 and sell them at $2, you return the original shares and keep the difference. People do this because it can be an excellent way to earn money and make your net income look and seem higher than it was.

If you own a company, you can leverage the business's equity to get a loan. This will show less equity with your company, but your yearly profits will be much higher. If you do not own a business, then most likely you are looking into leverage for a higher return on stocks, or another type of investment, which can always be a great option!

Types of Insurance

Insurance is one of those topics that most people avoid talking about or sorting out, even though it is something every person should have. The same as you need to have car insurance, you need to have life insurance. There are always moments in people's lives that come at unexpected times, and if you are not properly prepared, this can cause a lot of issues for not only your life but your family's life too. In Canada, there are many different types of insurance for you to choose from, which means you have the option of finding the right insurance that fits your lifestyle.

When looking at insurance, it is normally branched off into two categories, Term Life Insurance and Permanent Life Insurance. Term Life Insurance ends after a certain date that was decided on when the insurance was set up, and only covers short-term needs. Term Life Insurance can be great because the premium (monthly payments) may be quite low compared to a more permanent solution.

The downfall to this type of insurance is that if you want to renew after the term is done, the monthly premium may increase by 3-5 times what it initially was, and it usually cannot be used past the age of 80. So, this type of a policy you would use to cover financial responsibilities earlier on in life such as specific things like mortgage, debt or a short time income replacement but a term insurance is not used for estate planning or charitable giving.

Permanent Life Insurance is exactly what is says; permanent! This type of insurance covers you for your entire life, and can even give you the opportunity to get some cash back while paying into the policy.

When it comes to Permanent Life Insurance, there are several branches of that. Whole Life Insurance is a type of permanent life insurance that gives you definite coverage for your whole life. Your payments (premiums) most likely will not change, which means that you will likely also be able to build some cash up within the policy. This type of insurance is great for people who want some kind of consistency with their payments.

Another form of Permanent Life Insurance is Universal Life Insurance. This is a more flexible type of policy and offers different options, including premiums (payments) or benefits that can all be adjusted to fit your needs. The major difference between Whole Life Insurance and Universal Life Insurance is that universal insurance has the option to include payment into a tax shelter to be used later, so you can customize your policy, whereas, with whole life insurance, everything is more concrete.

This type of life insurance also has an investment account, which does equal a certain amount of money. In some cases, you will be able to take loans out of the said account, although this option isn't for everyone. If you are looking for more of a customized form of life insurance, then this policy could work well for you!

Ok!! YOU DID IT! You got through the financial terms!!

There are so many options for you when it comes to making an investment! Whether you want something long-term or short-term, or whether you want to invest a lot or only a little, the options are endless. Do not let any of these terms confuse you because, as much as this all seems like a lot to remember, it can be pretty simple, and I am here to help you along the way.

Let's get that extra money into your pockets and set up the perfect plan for you to invest in your future!

Homework

1) Make a list of the types of places you have money

2) Make a list of your interest rate beside each type of place

3) Make a list of the fees your paying beside each type of place

Optional 4) Send me your list and any questions you have

THE "B" WORD IS NOT A BAD WORD

Don't spend time beating on a wall, hoping to transform it into a door.

- Coco Chanel, French fashion designer

Manage your spending by creating and sticking to a budget.

- Alexa Von Tobel, CEO of LearnVest.com

Yes, ladies, we are talking about the "B" word! No, not the one you are thinking about, but that other word some people are not too fond of; budgets! For some reason, a lot of people avoid making budgets because they either think it is a waste of time, or they do not know how to make one properly and stick to it, or they are really concerned that making a budget means they have to cut out all the 'fun' in their lives.

I think of budgets like diets; sometimes they are needed to get you back on track, then you can eat an entire chocolate cake. But don't actually eat a whole cake on my advice! Budgets are great because they give you an opportunity to track your money, so you are able to visually see where your money is going and ways to save so you don't have to live paycheque to paycheque.

I love creating a budget because it clearly shows you how you can allocate money and also provides you with a clear amount of what you can spend on the fun stuff.

Create The Budget You Need

Creating a proper budget can take a little bit of time, but, when you stick to it, it is such a beneficial thing to have in your life. Whether you have a plan to save a certain amount of money, or you just want to keep better track of your money, a budget can help you. Many people nowadays have trouble saving money because there is always that next thing to buy or the next item you want. I promise a budget makes your life easier. You won't lose sleep worrying if bills are paid, or worry about how much is in your bank accounts, or how much you have spent the past month because you will always know.

When starting to look into budgets, start by looking at your income (how much you make). This can include any employment income, any investments, spousal/child support, really any money that you receive. Then you want to take a look at all your costs. Costs include mortgages, rent, credit card bills, and any other payments you are consistently making. If you have any major purchases to be made in the near future, add those in so you are better prepared and know how much money you will have after the purchase. Remember, some of these costs, or even the money you are receiving, may change, so this is really a guideline to follow. But, if you are looking to stay on track with your finances, a budget is an excellent way to do so!

There are quite a few different options when it comes to setting up a budget. You can look up templates for them, or you can even get someone, like me, to create one for you. If you are looking up a template for creating your budget, look it over to make sure it is the right fit for you. Some templates have specific expenses that you may not have, so find something that is personalized around your own lifestyle. Microsoft Office has some great budget templates that are easy to use, and all you need to do is enter your expenses and your incoming amounts of money. All templates can be customized; just do some research and find one that is a good fit for you.

A lot of people look at Excel spreadsheets for creating a budget because they are simple, and automatic calculations can be set up within the spreadsheet, so there is less work for you in the end. Excel is a great resource that is fairly simple to use, and also has tons of options and specifications to plan a budget for you and your family.

Another option is getting someone else to do a budget for you. There is nothing wrong with hiring someone to plan out a budget for you. If you have a busy lifestyle, and cannot find the time, then this may be the only option for you. This is definitely a more expensive choice, but you know it will be done properly and will be tailored to your lifestyle.

Do not fear the budget! If you want to track your finances and know exactly how much money you have at any given time, a budget can really help make all of that easier. Just be realistic and honest with yourself so you are not making a budget that has no use to your lifestyle, and you will be well on your way!

Worksheets

A worksheet is a great way to get that budget on paper instead of inside your head. It is basically physical proof of your budget and gives you a reference to look at. Many people think they can keep track of their finances without writing anything down, and while there may be some people who are able to do that, the majority of people are not as lucky! Worksheets give you the options of simplifying your life and giving yourself a visual resource to see how much money you have and how much you will need to cover all your expenses.

There are so many different options when it comes to creating the perfect worksheet for you! Even doing a google search, can you give you hundreds of choices. There are free templates you can download and print so you can simply jot down all of your expenses and keep a copy of it on hand, so you always have a reference to look back on. These are a great option if you are not as technologically advanced as others. All you would need to do is save the worksheet and print it out, then fill in your income and monthly costs.

Another option is to take the spreadsheet route and make a worksheet through that program. An advantage of using Excel is that you have the option of completely personalizing your worksheet, and also have the option of creating multiple worksheets on one file. If you have a very chaotic life, or even if you just have a lot of expenses, or different dates that all of these expenses are taken out; an excel worksheet can simplify all of this. If you have the time, make your worksheet the best it can be!

Think about it. If you have numerous different expenses, all of these add up, and it can actually get quite confusing if you have everything just stuffed onto one page. Having numerous worksheets can really spread out all your costs and make it less overwhelming to look at. Here is an example: If you have many costs contributed to transportation, you could then make a transportation worksheet and have everything related to that on a single page. That way, everything is related and you have no chance of confusion. If you are taking the route of having numerous worksheets, create a final worksheet that combines all the categories just so you have a main page that references all your costs and incoming money.

Try to keep in mind that making worksheets for a budget is not a one-time thing. This is something for you to look at on a regular basis to stay on track. Life gets complicated, and creating worksheets to simplify your life is really something everyone should be doing. Another reason why financial worksheets are usually not just something you glance at once or twice is because each year, costs go up. After a year, your costs for rent, bills, food, etc. will usually go up in price. I would recommend updating your budget quarterly. If anything changes, update it right away so you are not looking over something outdated and useless in your current life situation.

Creating worksheets can really benefit you and your life if you use them properly. Take the time and look over everything you spend your income on. Your best option is to organize your income and costs as much as you can. Create sub-categories, so you do not have a huge list of all your costs on one page. Do not complicate your life anymore than it needs to be; simplify it instead!

Household Expenses

Worksheets for budgets need to be simplified, not more complicated. That is why different sub-sections are created so you can take a better look at all your incoming and outgoing money. Household expenses are one of those sub-sections on your worksheet that are really necessary.

Whether you live in an apartment building, are paying a mortgage for a house, or have your house paid off, you are always going to have household expenses. Household expenses pertain to anything with your home, which usually includes either a mortgage or rent payment. Hydro, water, and any other type of utility that you pay for would also be included in this worksheet. If you pay for internet or cable, add this to the household expenses too.

Some of these expenses may be monthly costs, or costs that are not as frequent. If there are dates when these payments come out, add that on your worksheet, so you have no chance of forgetting. It is a good option to separate your expenses in regard to when payments are made and how often. This will also avoid some confusion. Make sections for weekly costs, monthly costs, yearly costs, and even one-time costs, just so you have a visual reference to see what you have paid or need to pay.

There are a few different types of expenses, but household expenses normally would fall under the category of a "fixed expense." This means that the cost of these expenses is not likely to change any time in the near future. These types of expenses are great for a budget because you will not need to update a lot when it comes to your household expenses.

Personal Expenses

Personal expenses are another sub-section in your budget that groups together all those costs that pertain to your personal life or your family's personal life. This includes anything that does not have anything to do with your home expenses. A Personal Expense worksheet is incredibly important because it gives you a guideline of what extra money you have (if any), and gives you a true idea of what you spend on a daily basis in your personal life.

Take a look at your life prior to making a budget. Do you have trouble saving money because there is always that next new thing you want? You may have trouble balancing your personal expenses. It is so hard to balance your life when it comes to having fun and working. You either overspend because you want to have an enjoyable life, and you want to make the people around you happy, or you spend all your time working because you are so wrapped up in having to pay off all your bills or attempting to save. This can make everything in your life incredibly stressful.

Start in the same way you did with your Household Expenses and start jotting down everything you spend money on in regards to your personal life. This can include clothing, food, toys for kids; anything that does not include paying for the household would go under Personal Expenses. Do not try to fudge the numbers to make your monthly income seem better than it actually is! This will not help you in any way and will actually make you feel pretty defeated because you will never catch up in life. Instead, be honest with yourself, and if you are overspending in a certain section, write it down, and see if there is anything you can do to resolve that issue.

When looking into your income for personal expenses, it is recommended to use only types of income that are consistent and stable. Adding money in that you "may" get, or a raise that is coming up does not help your current budget because that is not what you are making. If you have made an investment and would like to keep track of it, make a separate worksheet for that so you can still look into the investment, but it is not blended in with income that stays the same.

The majority of your personal expenses are going to be considered "Discretionary Spending." This is when you have money that is used towards things that are more wanted than needed. There are some types of discretionary spending that are definitely necessary, like groceries, which are obviously something needed rather than something just wanted.

It may be a good option to spend some time tracking your spending habits to see how often you are spending money on items that are more of a want than a need. This way, if you take that time, you may realize costs that can be eliminated, and you can make a budget that both properly fits your lifestyle, and gives you options on how to save your money better!

The Power of Tracking and Habits

Keeping track of what is going on in your life should be an automatic, normal task for you to want to partake in. The same as you set your alarm to wake up the next morning, or you have the same routine each night before going to bed. Those habits developed from practice and unconscious tracking. Tracking your money will become fun too. Tracking your life and your spending is how you can get yourself ahead and be back on track when it comes to money. So many people avoid making budgets because of the amount of work that goes into it. Yes, it may take a bit of time to track your spending, but it really does pay off in the end!

Habits can be tough to break, but it is so rewarding when you actually succeed. If you want to change your lifestyle, and have a better grip on your life, get into the right habits. Make a habit of staying on track with your financial situation instead! Get into the habit of saving as much money as possible instead of spending as much as you can. This way, looking down the road, you have a much higher chance of having money saved.

Use the 21/90 rule, it takes 21 days to build a habit, and it takes 90 days to make it a lifestyle. Tracking daily for 21 days will help you get into a habit of realizing where your money grows and goes; continuing to track for 90 days will help you build a lifestyle of money recognition.

If you are doing your money tracking and budgeting on your own, then make a routine of it. I recommend daily tracking! Before you wind down for the evening, record everything you spent for that day on a budget sheet. Looking at your finances and budgets at the same time every day and week will help it to stay consistent and turns it into more of a routine rather than a chore.

If you would like to hire me to keep track of your finances, we will keep your money meetings short and frequent because if the meetings are too long, they will feel like a chore, and you are likely to stop having them. If you don't hold them frequently enough, it's hard to turn it into a habit. We need to have that healthy balance!

Making a habit of something, especially finances and creating a proper budget for yourself, can be tough, but it gives you the opportunity to feel free from stress because you actually have a plan set in place. Don't let it overwhelm you, just take it one step at a time, and before you know it, you will be well on your way to saving money and being in a better financial situation than you could ever have imagined!

Homework

1) Take a sheet of paper and divide it into 3 columns; Income/Fixed Expenses/Other Expenses. Record on the sheet all the things that are included in each of these sections.

2) Track your daily spending for seven days, including everything you spend money on, even the littlest piece of gum.

3) On a calendar write out all your fixed expenses dates and your income dates

4) At the end of the week, transfer your weekly total to the week/month tracker

5) Are you happy with the amount you spend and the amount you save each month? If not, please contact me, and we'll discuss ways to fix it.

*All expense sheet options are available on the website.

BENEFITS OF LIVING

Be thankful for what you have; you'll end up having more

If you concentrate on what you don't have, you will never, ever have enough.

- Oprah Winfrey, American Executive

Savings

Did you know that if you leave $10,000 in the bank, it will take approximately 36 years for you to have $15,000, but the bank will make an average of $300,000-$7,000,000 from investing your money? The bank uses your deposit money to loan it to other people at a higher interest rate than what they offer you. The amount of interest the banks collect on loans is greater than the interest they pay you, so the difference is the bank's profit. Also, the amount of fees you are charged each year is profit for the bank. The fees and interest you pay can make it quite difficult to be able to save properly. Do you want to let the bank make all the money, or would you like to become the bank?

There are many different types of savings, but most people only go to a bank to find out which one is best for them. Finding the right one for you can be tricky due to all the options out there. Banks offer a variety of savings accounts, depending on what you are looking for. Their fees can be pretty low, but they can go higher, based on if and how often you take money out of the account. The interest rates are not overly high, so this is not the best option if you are looking to have your money grow.

Another option for saving your money is to put it into a high-yield bank account. These bank accounts do have the option of higher interest rates, which will give you a greater chance to earn more money. However, the way many banks are structured, you will most likely have to put down a larger deposit than most savings accounts when opening your high-yield bank account.

You can also use a TFSA, but as mentioned in Chapter 4, TFSA are ideally used as an investment platform rather than a bank account. A bank will offer you whatever their current interest rate is, whereas an investment company will structure a TFSA to meet your financial goals.

Everyone is different, which is why there are so many options to choose from when it comes to saving your money. What you want to do is keep your financial independence number (FIN) in mind for long term savings plans and for short term savings, find a savings account that can get you the best return, but without all the ridiculous fees. If you are unsure, start small, and go for a savings plan that is short term, so that if those funds need to be accessed, you will not be charged an excessive amount of fees.

Even if you are just looking to save a little more money because you overspend, there are ways to do so. For most of my clients, we look at money-in-money-out bank savings account for everyday and routine monthly expenses, with the lowest fees and likely little to no interest, as well as a second savings account for larger purchases that will be in the next year. When looking at anything longer than one year, I help my clients set up investment portfolios based on their long-term dreams and goals.

If you are concerned about where all that money is going or whether you should make that purchase or save your money, try looking at pending purchases based on how many hours you worked to get that item. For example, if you want to buy a new pair of shoes instead of putting that money into savings, think about how many hours you had to do your hard work, and then consider whether or not purchasing that item is really worth it.

For example, a $100 purchase, if you make a $20/hour, means you work for five hours to afford that item. Most of the time, you are going to want to put the item down because you will see the value of your work and the importance of putting that extra money into savings, so you have the opportunity to earn more for your future.

Inflation

Inflation is defined as certain items or services increasing over a certain amount of time. Some people are not aware, but the costs for pretty much anything you can think of has gone up so much in such a short period of time. Groceries, shelter, vehicles, gas, absolutely everything is drastically more expensive, and those costs only keep rising as time goes on. Whether you get a raise or minimum wage increases, it doesn't make a difference because the cost of living usually inflates more than your wages. There isn't a balance, so the balance tips to inflation, so you need to always be conscious of money habits.

When looking at inflation, it usually increases on a monthly or yearly basis, and gives you a better idea of how certain products will continue to inflate in upcoming years. There are normally three reasons for inflation.. One is that there is such a desire for a certain product that the cost of the product is raised because demands are so high. This is called demand-pull inflation. If a product is doing incredibly well, and the business has noticed a huge increase, then they may raise the cost of their product because the desire for the product is so strong.

The other reason for inflation to occur is something called cost-push inflation. This is when the cost for building or making the product rises, or the wages for workers goes up, and that causes the business or owner of products to inflate their prices. If a product is costing a company more than it previously did, then they are forced to charge more, or the company would end up losing money.

The last cause for inflation is wage-push inflation, and this is somewhat similar to cost-push inflation. This happens when a company's wages increase rapidly to the point where the costs for products need to be increased. Cost-push inflation can be caused by either minimum wage increasing or a company just increasing their wages in general. At many workplaces, when minimum wage increases, workers that receive more than minimum wage will also get a raise, so this will contribute to inflation occurring.

Let's take a look at some inflation changes over a span of 40 years. In 1975, costs for everything were dramatically lower than they are today, and families on average made a decent wage. The average family income was $50,000, whereas in 2015 it had gone up to $70,000. This doesn't seem like a large increase based on how much costs have gone up.

When looking at the average house price from 1975, it was about $60,000. This seems so low compared to the average cost of a house in 2015, which was about $700,000! Another shocking inflation change is tuition costs. In 1975, it was about $550 for tuition, whereas in 2015, it increased to $6,200, and each year it continues to increase.

All these inflation costs can make it seem impossible to be able to save because of the fact you always have to catch up. My recommendation is to never let yourself feel comfortable financially. If you feel like you have enough, take a second look at inflation, and you will quickly realize that you need to continuously save and have a budget so that you are able to keep up and protect your future.

If you are looking to keep up with all these inflation costs, the best advice is to look towards getting a yearly salary increase of 5%. A lot of companies offer yearly raises based on your work, so strive to do more to get that 5% increase, so you are not really affected by inflation. Obviously, this is not always an option for everyone, but there are other options to keep you out of debt and be able to afford all of your daily expenses.

Another way to protect yourself is to put your money into an investment, such as TFSA, Segregated Fund, Insurance, or Mutual Fund, which is going to give you an interest rate higher than the inflation rate. A financial professional can really help you take a look at your current income, your dreams and goals, your risk tolerance, and take into account yearly inflation so that you can stay on track and never fall behind with your money. Take a look at different types of investments in chapter 4 and find one that works best for you.

Living Benefit Insurance

Normally, when you think about life insurance, you assume it is something that is received after a person has passed away. This has usually been the case, but now life insurance has branched off into different options that benefit people who have not yet passed.

The living benefit insurance branches off into several different categories. The first one is disability insurance, which is for people who have injured themselves to the point of not being able to work. With disability insurance, the injury could have happened either at work or outside of work, and you can either get short-term or long-term insurance, depending on what you are looking for and what you are eligible for. Some employers may offer disability insurance in their group benefits, but it may only cover you if you are injured at work.

Independent disability insurance is recommended even if you have group benefits because the chances of you being injured at work are slim. Disability insurance will pay you monthly while you are disabled, and your payments will stop when you return to work. There are options for everyone regardless of whether you have a group benefit plan or no benefits at all; there are policies that you can apply for.

Another type of living benefit insurance is called critical illness insurance. This type of insurance is normally used when a serious unexpected illness is diagnosed. Critical illness will pay you a lump sum amount to be used as you need it. There really aren't limitations regarding how this money can be used, but most people use it to help pay bills, pay for non-covered medical treatments, or any caregiver costs. Some examples of illnesses that can be covered through critical illness insurance are cancer, heart attack, stroke, Alzheimer's, and kidney failure.

Think of an elder who can no longer care for themselves; long-term care insurance may be something they should have put in place. This is a type of benefit that normally pays monthly to someone who needs to be placed in a care facility. To be eligible for this type of benefit, your reasoning for being in a care facility would have to be due to no longer being able to care for yourself without some assistance. This benefit will help cover the costs to stay in a care facility, as well as cover your own personal costs whenever they come up. As long as you are over 40, and do not make enough after retirement to cover all costs, then you could be eligible.

One of the most well-known types of living insurance is travel insurance, and this is set up just in case something happens while you are travelling and need help to cover any medical costs. It is recommended that before travelling, you set up travel insurance because you never know what could happen, and it is better to be fully prepared than not at all.

Heath and dental coverage is another well-known type of living insurance. This is another one that may be covered by your place of work through group benefits, but can also be set up through private insurance companies. This type of insurance is to cover any health or dental costs that happen to come up. Medications and certain types of treatments, especially dental, can cost a lot of money, and if they are recurring, then eventually all those treatments can put you into debt. This is another great option to keep you fully prepared just in case anything unexpected happens.

Marriage

Have you been planning your dream wedding your whole life? Or if you are already married, were you completely blown away by the total cost of your wedding? There are so many costs contributing to weddings that can really break the bank and make a not so pleasant start to a marriage if you are going into it already in debt. The wedding is just the initial cost of a marriage. And when it comes to money and learning how to properly budget, if you and your partner are not on the same page, then that marriage may not last very long if you both do not put in the effort.

Let's take a closer look at those shocking wedding costs to see, on average, how much you are spending prior to even getting married and settling down. If you do not have a large enough property of your own, then you will most likely have to book a venue; this does not normally come cheap! On average, you will probably be spending around $10,000 just on the location for your wedding.

Then, there is the dress, the suit, and the outfits for bridesmaids and groomsmen, which is about another $5,000. You are already at $15,000, and that doesn't even include food, entertainment, and decorations. If you are not careful and have no money in savings for this special occasion, then you are at risk of causing some marital problems before the marriage even begins!

Once they are married, most couples want to take some time away to go on a honeymoon, and this is just another added cost. On an average income, there is no possible way you can cover all of these purchases without going into debt. That is why budgeting and saving are so important at any point in your life.

After all that fun and excitement of getting married and having your honeymoon, reality sets in, and you then have to be on the same page with someone financially. For a lot of people, that can be a tough task. What if you married someone who spends more than what you actually have? What if they do not agree with your budget and choose to do what they want with their money? These scenarios can cause a lot of marital problems if you are not careful.

Money problems can put so much stress on an individual person, let alone a growing family that already has its own stressors. This is why it is recommended to discuss money prior to getting married to really know what you are getting into.

Children

Did you know that if you have kids, on average, you will spend about $243,660 by the time they turn 18 years old? That equals out to $12,825 each year, and only for one child. Most families have two or three children, so multiply $243,660 by 3, and that totals the shocking number of $730,980! Parents do not think about this total while following their daily routines, but children cost a lot of money, and if you do not plan ahead of time and have some money saved, then you could put yourself in a large amount of debt.

Before even having children, you have to plan and put a lot of money towards your family's future. When you become pregnant, you have nine months to purchase a large stock of baby furniture, clothing, diapers; the list is never-ending. Not only do you have to make all these purchases, but once you have your child and go on maternity leave, you will most likely not be getting the full income that you normally would receive from work.

Some workplaces, depending on how long you have been there, will offer maternity leave, but most people end up applying for employment income maternity leave. This is a great option for you if your workplace does not offer maternity leave because it still gives you the chance to have money coming in, but the downside of it is that the maximum amount EI can give you is $485 a week. This can make it incredibly tricky to put money away or even have enough to cover all costs.

Moneysense.ca states that for every year you take off (usually in regards to maternity leave), you end up with a 3% loss in wages. So, if you think about it, if you have three kids, you could have lost 9% of your wage just from taking time off. Once you do return back to work, you then have to take into account that child care costs a lot of money. There are subsidy options for certain households, but you must have a lower level of income to qualify for this option. Sometimes families are working just to be able to afford child care, especially if no money is saved ahead of time.

Child care may be expensive, but it is definitely a lot cheaper than tuition costs. Most parents start a savings plan for their child's education right when they are born so that when they turn 18, they have the majority of their tuition covered. While there is the option of your child applying for government-supported loans, it then puts your child in debt, so either way, it's a large cost that is necessary for your child's/children's future.

I received a loan through the Ontario Student Assistance Program (OSAP) for my post-secondary education; it took me nine years to pay it back. Setting up a Registered Education Savings Plan (RESP) while children are young is an ideal way to set some money aside and obtain some of the government funding.

These costs just keep growing as your family keeps growing. Clothing is a huge expense as kids are constantly getting bigger. Parents cheer when their kids are out of diapers just for the simple fact that that is no longer a purchase they have to make! The best way to make sure you always have enough money to cover everything is to stick to your budget and build your emergency fund, so you are not panicking at the start or the end of each month.

Long-Term Investment Perspective

The cost of waiting can cause serious problems for your financial future. It is much better that you get started saving today, even if it is a small amount so that you can build bigger wealth for your future. The earlier you choose to start saving, the more your money will grow, and you have a much better chance at having the life you want. Do you remember the rule of 72 and the benefits of compound interest?

Each year, most types of investments have very fluctuating results. If you have a short-term investment and are constantly keeping track of it, that can cause a lot of nervousness on your end because you see the numbers go up and down so quickly. A long-term investment will do the same, but because it is long-term, those constant fluctuations in the fund will not seem as drastic compared to a short-term investment that does not give you a lot of time to have your money increase.

A long-term investment obviously needs a lot more time, but the money you get out of that investment is worth it. These investments will fluctuate, but that is normal when dealing with the financial market. When you are looking at long-term investments, think about what you need the money for. What is the future plan for this investment? This way, you can get the right one that will give you the best result.

Take a look below to see how much you could have coming your way depending on when you start saving:

	Age 23	Age 32
Salary $32,000		
Initial contribution 5%	$1600	$1600
Monthly contribution	$100	$100
Annual interest	7%	7%
Retirement age 65	$314,574	$118,585

Now, try to consider a much bigger picture, and increase your contribution by just 2% each year. Your savings at retirement would increase to $508,361 if you were to start at age 23. If you started at 32, they would increase to $253,482.

There is no wrong age to start saving, but when you start at an age closer to retirement rather than earlier on in life, you have a much lower chance of having enough money to cover your lifestyle once you do choose to retire. When you're young and just starting out in your field of work, you normally are not thinking about saving for retirement or putting your money into a long-term investment, but this is something everyone should do.

Putting your money into some kind of investment is the best option you can make to guarantee a stress-free life after retirement. If you want the best life for yourself, start looking at investments and life insurance early. Prepare yourself instead of having to figure it out later on in life when it is truly needed.

Homework

1) Make a list of the types of banking accounts you have.

2) What fees and interest rates do you have for each account?

3) What type of living benefits insurance do you have? How much? What is the claim criteria?

4) What is your long-term investment perspective? Such as your FIN, are you on target? Are you prepared if your needs change? Such as getting married, children, post-secondary education, divorce, illness or injury

WHEN THERE IS TOO MUCH (OR TOO LITTLE)

You must gain control over your money, or the lack of it will forever control you.

- Dave Ramsey, businessman

Meeting Dreams and Goals

Many people make a list of dreams and goals to help them stay on track and see what they can achieve as they work towards those goals. It is the reward for the work done. It makes you see a purpose for all the effort you put in on a daily basis to save for your future. Have you ever made a list of your dreams and goals? If you have not, why do you think that is?

Writing down your dreams and goals can be a great way to start when it comes to having the life and future that you want. Go back to Chapter 3; what were your top 3? If you are unsure about major dreams and goals, then start small. You do not want to write down a dream or goal that is clearly unrealistic, as that will just make you unsure of the path you are on. For example, writing down that you want to become the Queen of England; is a great goal, but looking at the big picture, that is most likely never going to happen.

Create goals that mesh well with your lifestyle. If you eventually want to be out of debt, find a timeline that works for you and jot that down as one of your goals. I recommend breaking it up into 90-day timelines so you can stay on track. Creating timeliness is not something to do quickly in one day. Spend some time on this, and realistically think about how long each dream or goal will take until you will be able to check it off the list. Having a timeline next to the goal will help you stick with it and not give up because you will see an actual date to make this happen.

When it comes to the timelines of goals, you do not want to put a rush on it. There is no reason to make yourself overwhelmed over something that should be a positive thing. Some dreams or goals will take longer than others, but do not feel defeated if your list takes longer than you were anticipating. Every task, whether small or large, takes time, but in the end, it is so worth it. If you don't step forward, you'll always be in the same place.

Some goals will have numerous steps, depending on how high you are aiming. If it is a huge dream or goal you have, then there may be different aspects of it that you need to achieve before it all comes together. If one of your goals is to be out of debt before the age of 50, then you will need to jot down numerous steps on how you will achieve that dream/goal. If you owe money to different companies or people, then write those down and create a separate timeline to show you when each of those debts will be paid off. There are tools on the website to help track your total debt and break down the amount you pay until you are debt-free.

Debt Management

Simple debt management strategies can include giving up small luxuries for a period of time and putting that money towards your debt. I use this strategy often, and I have taught it to my children. There are many times it would be easier to get a coffee on the go, get my nails done, or get my hair professionally dyed, but I negotiate with myself to see what I am sacrificing to do so. If I have bought new shoes, clothes, or a purse, can I put off getting my hair done this month and instead buy a $15 hair dye and do it myself so I can put the $100 it would have cost me at the salon, onto my credit card instead?

The tricky thing with debt management is that the minimum payment you see on a statement is a lot less than what you are paying in interest. Often it is 2%-5% of your balance. For example, one of my clients had a credit card with $8,000 owing on it. She was diligent at paying the minimum amount as her statement requested, which was 3% of her $8000 at $240. IF she continued to pay just the minimum, she would pay $3,464.80 in interest, and it would take her 48 months to pay it off.

So instead of just paying $8,000, she would have paid a total of $11,464.80. Instead, we figured out a budget that she could cut out a few other things and put an additional $40 a month onto her credit card. Just by making this small change, she would be able to pay off the credit card in 38 months instead and save $729.60 in interest charges.

There are different theories on how to pay off debt, one being the snowball method that you pay off the accounts with the smallest balances first while paying the minimum payments on the larger debts, or the other is the avalanche method where you pay off the highest interest rate first while paying the minimum on the lower interest rate debts. I love that each of these methods involves cold snow references, as that is often how you feel when you are struggling in debt. Sometimes debt can be very overwhelming, and restricting, consolidation, or bankruptcy may be needed.

Debt Restructuring versus Debt Consolidation

When your debt is too much to manage, you are losing sleep over it, or you have trouble making your monthly payments, debt restructuring or debt consolidation can give some peace of mind. Debt restructuring is about figuring out a payment plan that works for you, one that you can stick to, and then asking your creditors if the proposed payment plans are acceptable.

Often this is done through a company in that they reach out to creditors and arrange the payment plans. This could mean that you will be paying lower payments than they had originally asked for, to enable you to slowly pay off the balance owed and improve your credit. Usually, there is a fee for this service, but they also provide credit counselling to help you manage your finances after. My clients that have used this service have been overly happy with the results and have been very grateful for the support.

Another option is debt consolidation. The biggest difference is that debt consolidation involves getting a loan to pay off all your other debt so that you only have one payment to deal with and often at a lower interest rate than you would pay towards credit cards. In order to obtain a loan for debt consolidation, you need to have a decent credit score and some collateral such as a house.

While both debt restructuring and debt consolidation are great options to get your credit score better, get your finances back to how you want them, it is best to speak to a financial professional who can help you figure out what is best, based on your income and the debt that you have. Staying in that constant spiral of paying the bare minimum will not improve your credit, and you will be paying a lot more than is necessary, due to interest. There is no shame in getting help to improve your credit, and ultimately, your life. Simple steps can lead to a great future as long as you stick with it.

Bankruptcy

Personally, I consider bankruptcy as the last resort, but for some people, it is necessary. Bankruptcy is when the majority of your debts are removed, and you start fresh with the option of eventually rebuilding your credit. It is important to know that not all of your debts can be eliminated, and you may run the risk of losing your assets.

To be eligible for bankruptcy, you need to owe at least one thousand dollars, but most likely, you will not be approved for bankruptcy unless you owe over five thousand. You also need to show a pattern that you have been unable to pay off your debts, and you should have more debts than assets.

While filing for bankruptcy may seem like an option for you, there are several things to think about before making your final decision. First of all, if you have any assets such as a vehicle, or even your home, you could be at risk of losing them, depending on how much money you owe. Secondly, your credit score will dramatically decrease. If you are looking to improve your credit and create a better life for yourself, filing for bankruptcy may not be the right decision for you.

Many people are not aware of this, but once you file for bankruptcy, it will be noted on your credit report for six years, even after your bankruptcy has been discharged. And this will flag you to any lenders as being high risk, so this means it will be near impossible for you to obtain a credit card, a mortgage loan, or a car loan. Some debts that you have may not be removed when you file for bankruptcy, debts like student loans or those pertaining to taxes are unable to be erased. So, if or when you need to look into bankruptcy, check to see what types of debts you have so you are not spending time on something you may not be eligible for.

My preferences are debt restructuring first, then debt consolidation and finally bankruptcy if the other two aren't approved, but each person has different needs. When consulting a financial professional, you want to explore each option to see what fits best for you right now and especially for your future goals.

Money Needed at Retirement

When looking towards retirement, it can be a scary thought, wondering how you will be able to make your savings last until you pass away. Some people avoid the topic altogether because it is overwhelming knowing that they will not have a constant inflow of money like they had in the past while working. The earlier you start planning this out, the less stressful it will be in the end because you will actually be prepared.

The best place to start is to calculate exactly how much money you will need to save to get you through your retirement without worry. The best way to do this is to take a look at your living expenses. This includes a mortgage or any household payments, food, clothing, transportation, and any other bills you will need to pay. You also want to take a look at inflation to see if that's something you should make adjustments for. Even basic costs like food and clothing get affected by inflation, so it is always best to be realistic and make those basics costs a little higher than normal, just to be safe. Remember your financial independence number?

Since you will no longer be working and will have a lot of extra time on your hands once you retire, you will most likely spend more money on new activities or hobbies. Having all that spare time will make it so you will want to go out and explore or try new things. Not only will you want to have extra money for new hobbies, but you may also need some spare money just in case of any health problems. As you get older, certain issues may arise, and a lot of treatments can cost you quite a bit of money. You never know what could happen, so it is best to be as prepared as you possibly can be.

A lot of individuals or couples like to travel when they reach retirement. This can be very costly, depending on how often you plan on travelling, so that is something that needs to be taken into account. If you plan on taking a yearly trip, you'll want to calculate every expense that would be included in the trip to get an annual cost for travel. Then, you can calculate how much money you would need in total for travel costs when retiring.

Try to be as specific as possible. Figure out how many days you plan to travel for, and where you will be staying. Write down every single cost to avoid overspending, so you have a much higher chance of having all the money you will need throughout retirement.

As morbid as it is to plan, it is also recommended that you have the costs of your passing and funeral costs all ready to go. An average funeral in Canada costs about $50,000. Cemetery costs are $18,000-$25,000 and increasing by 10% each year. And how much money do you plan on leaving to your loved ones after you pass? A lot of these costs will be included in your will so that a lawyer can go over everything with family members and loved ones.

This will not only lower your stress because you will have everything planned out, but it will also reduce your loved ones' stress levels because they will not have to figure out how to cover everything when you pass, and will then be able to grieve instead of worrying about all the funeral costs and getting it all prepared.

To fully maximize the amount of money you will get for retirement, you should invest your money to give you the best chances of having more than you need once you choose to retire. There are many different options for you to invest, so do not rush, and find one that will give you the best payout once it is closed. You should also take a look at your Canadian Pension Plan prior to retirement so that you know ahead of time how much you will be receiving but keep in mind that government programs may not be there when you retire, so don't count on that being your only source of income at retirement.

A good rule of thumb is to plan to withdrawal 6% each year from your retirement money, and then you won't run out of money as long as your investment interest rate is 6% or higher. So, what that means is if you want to live on $30,000 yearly in retirement, you will need about $500,000 saved at age 65, and if you want to live on $60,000, you will need to save about $1,000,000. These are estimated amounts, so it's best to have exact numbers reviewed with a financial professional.

If you are still concerned that you will not have enough to cover your full retirement, then there are other options. Just because you retire doesn't mean you cannot work a part-time job. Sometimes it is not possible due to health, but it is a great way to earn some extra income and keep your stress levels low because you always know more money is coming in.

Another great way to save money is to see if moving to a cheaper location is a better option for you. Depending on where you are located, there could be lower taxes in a different area, or even the cost for a home may be cheaper, so it is definitely a great option if you are looking to save a little more money.

There are so many options for you when it comes to retiring, so take some time and look through all the information that is available to you. Keep in mind that some things such as investments, insurance, and mortgage may cost you money now, but it's preparing you for a stress-free retirement. The earlier you figure all this out, the more time you have to properly save for your retirement.

Taxes

As time goes on, more and more people are taking the simple route and going to a company to do their taxes for them. Not that there is anything necessarily wrong with that, but I would recommend going to a certified tax expert who can maximize your money.

Taxes were created essentially to pay for all the necessary services that help us in our daily lives. They are used to help pay for road repairs, our health care, schools, and so much more. When you pay your taxes, you are helping not only yourself but everyone around you. They are set in place to make positive changes where you live.

Depending on where you are located, taxes may be sorted out differently, but in Canada, when you complete your taxes they are always sent and processed through Canada Revenue Agency (CRA). You complete your taxes on an income tax form that will then get sent to the CRA for them to review. There are four different ways you can send your tax return. You can send it electronically, on paper in the mail, on the phone, or you can get a tax preparation company to fill out your tax return for you. When you have a lower quality tax company complete your taxes, there is a chance something will be missed and you will end up owing more money than originally calculated; a tax expert such as a CPA would be beneficial.

When doing your taxes, you first want to make sure that all of your personal information is updated so that there is no chance of an audit popping up in your future. If you have a change in your marital status, make sure to inform CRA as soon as that change has occurred. If you have had a child, you are then entitled to certain benefits, so it is important to let them know that as it can affect your chance of getting any benefits like GST or the Child Tax Credit.

The next step in completing your taxes is reporting any income you made the year prior. This can include income from your workplace, or if you have your own business, you would include that amount of income. Even if a job was temporary, or just a side job, it needs to be reported. You need to make sure to also include any investments you have made as that can affect your return.

Once all your income is reported, you then have to claim any deductions, tax credits, or expenses you had that can offer a tax break. These credits and deductions can actually help you pay less back on your tax return. If you are married or common-law, there may be some family credits available to you. If you have children, and you have custody, you are eligible to receive tax credits that will lower the amount you owe, and you also have the option of applying for certain benefits that can give you extra money throughout the year.

Another deduction that you may be qualified to receive is in regard to education. If you went to college or university and are currently paying off your tuition, there may be credits you are eligible to receive. If you have completed school and are now working, there are plenty of tax credits that you should take a look at to see if there is anything you can claim. Try to make a habit of saving all your receipts, so there is proof of your expenses. If you do not save receipts, there is no way to prove you are entitled to certain tax credits or deductions. There are so many different tax breaks; you just have to do your research to see exactly what you are eligible to receive.

Once your tax return is completed, you can either send it electronically, which is usually the fastest option, over the phone, or by mail. Sending it in the mail is probably the slowest option because many people still choose to send their returns this way, and processing takes time. When the CRA processes your return, it typically takes on average 6-8 weeks, depending on how it was sent and when you are sending it. All of Canada usually sends their taxes around the same time, so there can be a longer delay depending on how busy the Canada Revenue Agency is with processing other returns.

Once it has been processed, you will receive your Notice of Assessment in the mail, or online depending if you have a CRA account set up. This will let you know if there were any issues when completing your return, as well as if you are receiving any refund. If there is money still owed to CRA after your tax return is completed, there are ways to pay them back, whether it is a payment plan or paying it off immediately. The option is all yours, although it is recommended you pay it off immediately to avoid any extra fees.

Insurance

When planning your future, you also want to look at insurance. If you had a toaster that popped up $5000+/month, would you insure it for a $100/month in case it broke? How do you know if you have too much or too little? As mentioned in chapter 4, term insurance is only for a certain period of time and will be completely gone when the term is finished. But what about permanent insurance? It is set in place for your entire life, but how do you know if you have the right amount?

The quick rule for permanent insurance is to have 10-20 times your income, depending on your debt. If you have a large amount of debt, you want to consider adjusting that number to 20-30 times your income just to be sure you have enough to cover everything. The other thing to keep in mind is if you have life insurance with your employer, that insurance will not follow you when you are no longer at work.

You also want to take into account your dependents and loved ones. Your life as a single person drastically changes when you get married, or have children, so your insurance may need to be adjusted based on this factor. If you have a mortgage with your spouse, you want to make sure both of you have enough life insurance so that if anything happens to the other person, you are confident that the bills can still be paid. Families are more likely to have debt compared to someone with a single person's income and lifestyle, so it is also recommended to look at insurance that helps cover those costs, so your loved ones are not required to pay off your debt after you're gone.

Remember insurance is used for three main things:

1) To cover your debt

2) To replace your income for your family

3) Cost of your final expenses

Life insurance may seem unnecessary when you are healthy and just starting out your career life, but that is the best time in your life to set it up. The main reason is that you never know what will happen, and setting up life insurance will guarantee you will have enough money insured to cover all your costs. I know you don't want to leave your loved ones to have to worry about how to pay bills and survive without your income. Plan ahead and give your family the best chance at having a stress-free life.

Homework

1) Review your FIN and your dreams

2) Review your debt and what is your best option to pay it down.

3) Write down how you envision your retirement lifestyle. How much money do you need to live on each year in retirement?

4) Calculate how much insurance you need.

(Income x 10 or 20) + Debt + Funeral expenses= total insurance amount

MORTGAGE AND REAL ESTATE ... WHAT DO I NEED?

Working hard for something we don't care about is called stress.

Working hard for something we love is called passion.

- Simon Sinek, Author

For the average person buying a home, it is rare that the home can be paid for immediately in full; usually, a mortgage loan is required. A mortgage gives you the option to still have the home you want, but not have all those upfront costs that would normally make it impossible to purchase your home. While many homeowners have a mortgage, not all of them know what having a mortgage really means or understand all the extra costs that come along with it.

Major components of the Mortgage

People just starting out in their careers, and purchasing their first home can become very unsure and confused with all the definitions and costs that come with a mortgage; it is a lot to remember! Do not worry if you feel like a fish out of water; there are professionals to help you, but it is important to at least know the major components of the mortgage.

When looking at your mortgage, you want to know the face value, which is the total amount of money that was borrowed from the lender. It is the total amount that you have to repay. This does not include interest or fees; it is only the total cost of the amount you initially borrowed.

The next component you want to be aware of is the term. This is how long you have until all payments have to be made. After that time, the mortgage either must be paid in full, including all fees and interest, or you will have to renew with the current lender or switch to a new lender. Terms usually range from six months to ten years, but most terms are about five years. Choosing what term is best for you depends on how much you want to put down on your payments, and how quickly you want your mortgage to be paid off. If you have a shorter term, then you must make higher payments, but you will not have to make as many payments. If you have a longer term, you will have smaller payments, but may end up paying more interest because you are making payments for a longer period of time.

An amortization period is somewhat similar to a term, and it describes the number of years it will take to repay the total amount that you borrowed. This includes both the initial total cost (principal) and the interest that will have accumulated. This is something that is calculated by the lender, and it will give you a proper schedule as to when payments need to be made and when the total loan will be paid off. When dealing with interest-only mortgages, you do not have to worry about amortization periods because the initial cost is not taken into consideration until the interest payments are completed.

Remember that I mentioned banks make their profits by lending your cash deposits to others and charging interest. Well, a mortgage is one of the larger interest money making products they have. Another important component that is quite simple to understand is the interest rate. This refers to the percentage of interest that you need to pay, on top of the initial cost of your mortgage. The percentage of interest will be calculated into payment amounts based on the cost of your home. This term should be something you should always be aware of, so you are able to pay off your mortgage as quickly as possible.

A compounding frequency is actually connected to both the interest rate and the term; think of the Rule of 72. This is the number of times interest is calculated based on the amount left owing on your principal loan. This is usually done either semi-annually or annually and can help you have lower interest rates depending on how much has been paid off on the total cost of the loan.

Another important thing you should know when it comes to your mortgage is high ratio vs conventional mortgage. A conventional mortgage is when you get a loan for 80% of the total cost of your property, and you pay a 20% down payment. A high ratio mortgage is when the lender is giving a loan that is over 80% of the total cost of your property. This means the borrower would have to make a down payment of less than 20%.

If you do decide to go with the high ratio mortgage and are approved, you will have to get mortgage default insurance on your mortgage loan, usually through either Canadian Mortgage and Housing Corporation or Genworth Financial. Mortgage Default Insurance is something you need to have if you don't have a 20% down payment, but this insurance doesn't protect you. This is only to protect the lending company, in case you aren't able to make payments and you default on your loan.

You still require mortgage life insurance, which is used to pay off your mortgage balance in the event of you or your partner's death. For most client's I see we protect them through life insurance, critical illness insurance and disability insurance so that the mortgage payments are covered, and then they don't need additional mortgage life insurance.

Loan to value ratio (LTV).is something that lenders will calculate before approving a mortgage. It is quite a simple formula that you can do at home just so you are aware when applying for a mortgage. The formula is your mortgage amount (how much the banks will lend you) divided by the appraised property value (how much your home is worth), and this will be calculated into a percentage.

Here is an example. If you have a $200,000 home with 5% down payment of $10,000, it would be a high ratio mortgage with an LTV of 95%. This percentage will determine if you are eligible for either a conventional or high ratio mortgage.

The Costs of Having a Mortgage

Before taking the steps towards looking for a house and getting a mortgage, you should first take a look to see if you are even eligible to get approved. A proper pre-approval is done so that you know the maximum amount of a mortgage that you can afford, an estimate of the payments, and also gives you an opportunity to lock in an interest rate for 60 days. Hint: an online 'quick' quote from various institutions does not always guarantee you're pre-approved and may damage your credit score. I recommend sitting with a licensed mortgage broker to get a proper pre-approval.

Once you are ready to get a mortgage, there are three key areas when it comes to mortgage basics; your credit rating, the property you plan to purchase, and the type of mortgage you choose.

The first of those key areas is your credit rating. The bank you are dealing with will take a look at your credit report. In your credit report, they are looking for your payment history to look for any payments you have missed, either recently or in the past. Missed payments can show that you are unable to make consistent payments, and that can affect your chances of getting a mortgage for your home. Your credit report will also show if you have any missed payments that have gone to a collection's agency, as well as bankruptcy.

The next key area to look at is the property you plan on getting the mortgage for. You will need to know if you live in it, rent it out, or have someone live in a portion of it. Regardless of the type of property, it is a good idea to hire a home inspector who can really take a lot of the stress off of you, and make moving in a lot easier. An inspector will come into the home, and see if there are any damages, water damage in the basement, ceiling or walls, cracks in the foundation of the home, concerns with the insulation material, wiring, insect or rodent infestations, and many more things. Sometimes they will find nothing of concern, but it is better to be safe than sorry.

If all these steps are taken, and you are approved for a loan, the next step is figuring out which mortgage is for you.

Types of Mortgages

There are quite a few different types of mortgages for you to choose from, depending on what you are looking for. The most common type of mortgage is a fixed-rate mortgage. This type has a payment and interest rate that stay the same for the whole term. This type of mortgage is recommended if you want something consistent and want to pay the same amount every time. It is a great option because, even with interest rates rising, your payments will remain the same.

Another type of mortgage is a variable rate – fixed payment mortgage, and this simply means that the payments will remain the same, but the interest rates on those payments will fluctuate throughout the term of your loan. This is better for the lender, but not necessarily better for the person paying off the mortgage. This is because, as interest rates in general increase, so will the interest rates on your mortgage. If the market interest rates are low, then it can be a good option to go with a variable rate – fixed payment loan, but once the rates increase, then you can come into some issues if you are not on top of it.

Similar to the variable rate – fixed payment loan, the variable rate – variable payment has both fluctuating payments and interest rates. If the interest rate decreases, then your payment amounts will also decrease. Just like the other variable rate loan, this can be an excellent option when the interest rates are low because your payments are going to be lower than expected. However, once interest rates start increasing, your payment costs will also go up, so if you are looking for more of a fixed, consistent option, this may not be the right type of loan for you.

A less common option for a mortgage is called an interest-only loan. This is when the payments you make go strictly towards paying off your monthly interest rates. With this option, you are not building up the equity on your home as quickly as other loans, but it does give you the option of paying less in comparison to other loans. This usually isn't the best option because while you are paying off all the interest, you are not making payments towards the actual loan (the principal). If money is tight, this option is available, but it does not work long term because the principal still needs to be paid off.

Another type of mortgage is an interest accruing mortgage, which gives you the option of not paying any of the interest on your loan until your mortgage loan term has ended. This may seem like a great option because essentially, you are paying less, but once your term has ended, you then have to pay off all the interest that has been adding up. This is normally a short-term loan because of the amount of risk that comes with it, but it is there if someone deems it necessary.

Next up, we are going to take a look at the reverse mortgage. This is a type of interest accruing mortgage typically offered to seniors. It provides homeowners with up to 55% of their property value in a lump sum, less any current debt owed on the property. This amount accumulates interest until death, or until the property is sold (at which time the mortgage is due and payable).

To qualify for this type of mortgage, you need to be at least 55 years of age, and you must own, and live in, your own home. As well, you need to have your home pretty much paid off, or at least have a large amount of equity. This loan is great for people who do not want to sell their home but want to have a continuous supply of money.

The straight-line principal reduction mortgage is a repayment plan that allows the borrower to pay a set amount of principal each payment, along with accrued interest. This is a great option if you are looking to pay off your loan quickly. This may be beneficial to industries purchasing depreciating assets (equipment, vehicles), or individuals looking to own their home as fast as possible. The payments will be higher than most loans, but the benefit is that you have everything paid off much more quickly when compared to other mortgages.

Lastly, the graduated-payment mortgage gives you the choice of making lower payments in the beginning, which will increase over time, but it carries the risk of inability to make payments. This would be beneficial to someone who expects their income to increase over time, such as a newly formed business. This is why this type of loan is normally recommended for young people who are unable to make large payments, but will eventually be able to. The downside to this mortgage plan is that interest rates tend to be higher, which can make it difficult to pay off the actual loan.

For someone that already has a property there is an option called the Home Equity Line of Credit (HELOC), this type of loan gives you the option of using your home's worth to get a certain amount of money from the bank. You can borrow as much as your home is worth (depending on your lender), and as long as it is paid back within the amount of time set, then you can borrow again. This is a great option if you need a larger amount of money; however, if you do not make payments consistently, this can affect your chances of keeping your home.

Typical Interests Breakdown by Type

When looking at mortgages, there are quite a few different types, based on the amount of time to pay off the mortgage, and whether it is open, closed, or has a variable rate. An open mortgage means your payments are much more flexible, and there are no set dates for those payments to be made; the mortgage amount simply needs to be paid off at the end of the term. This gives you the option of paying when you want to, but it does normally have a higher interest rate because the payments are not set. With an open mortgage, you have two different options: 1 year or 6 months. This can be a great option if you plan on making a large payment that will pay off the majority of your loan. If money is tight, this may not be the best option for you.

A closed mortgage is when you have scheduled payments and normally will have the loan for the entire term. The advantage of having a closed mortgage is that interest rates will normally be lower because there is less risk to the lender. With a closed mortgage, you have an option of a 1-10-year mortgage, or there are options for zero down payment mortgages or cashback mortgages, depending on your interest rate.

The last type of mortgage is the variable rate mortgage. This type of loan has varying interest rates based on your total cost owed and the credit markets. Variable-rate mortgages will normally offer a lower interest rate, so it could help you pay less interest in the long run.

Why Apply for a Mortgage?

There are various reasons people or families end up applying for a mortgage loan. The most obvious reason for getting a mortgage is to assist you in purchasing your home. To obtain a mortgage usually requires a down payment and will have interest added to the loan. Many families need help in the purchase of a home because it is almost an impossible task to pay off a home immediately when the average cost is over $200,000.

Another reason someone may choose to apply for a mortgage is to refinance. This means they already have acquired a mortgage, but they want to increase the size of the mortgage on their existing property. If it is a closed mortgage, there will most likely be a penalty to pay. This isn't necessarily recommended, as it can put you in larger amounts of debt.

Equity take out (ETO) is when you increase the size of your mortgage by taking a second mortgage against the property, such as a HELOC. The borrower can use this money for any reason allowed by the lender, and may include: paying other debts or purchasing other assets (investments, vehicles, real estate). Again, this is not a recommended option, but if you need to pay off other debts, then this option is here for you.

Lastly, there is bridge financing, which is a method used when someone is selling their current home to buy a new one. If the closing date on the existing home is after the purchase date on the new one, a bridge finance scenario may be of benefit. This would result in a second mortgage being placed on the first home, while waiting for it to sell. Once the first home is sold, the mortgage is repaid, having provided a "bridge" between the two homes.

Extra Costs

Congratulations! You have now been approved for a mortgage! Here are some fees you need to be aware of that occur during the sale (closing) of your house purchase and full mortgage approval. For starters, there is something called a closing cost. A closing cost is the legal and administrative costs you will need to pay. This fee will be paid to your mortgage lender after the home has been purchased and is usually around 2-5% of the total cost of your home.

The next fee to take a look at is a real estate lawyer fee. When you buy a home, a real estate lawyer is the person preparing your documents to close on your home, so they will charge fees for things such as making photocopies, charges for mail delivery, filling out certain documents, and phone calls, which all help in the preparation and recording of official documents in order to legally purchase the home. A real estate lawyer will make sure the sellers can legally sell the house and ensure you aren't going to be responsible for expenses attached to the house. These fees in total can cost around $800-$1100 plus tax depending on what was needed from the lawyer.

Another fee is land transfer tax, which is something you pay to the government when you purchase your property. The fee amount for this varies by province, but the full cost of your home normally is looked at when figuring out the total amount of tax to pay. If you are purchasing a home for the first time, you may be able to apply to get a refund of land transfer tax.

There are a couple of extra costs that may not be necessary, but they are definitely beneficial to you; Registration of title and title insurance. Applying for registration of title is a fee that will show written proof that the property which you purchased is in your name. This can help you with any legal issues you may come across, and it can also help you when selling your home. This process can be quite lengthy depending on the time of year you are applying, but it is definitely a great document to have on hand.

Title insurance is often required by the mortgage lender to insure the property in case of a property owner dispute. This type of insurance can save you from various forms of problems including issues with previous homeowners having debts in regards to the home if someone is trying to take ownership of your home (title fraud), or any problems that could make it difficult for you to sell, or lease out your home. The cost of title insurance varies depending on the total cost of your home, but it is a one-time fee, and you will have the insurance for as long as you are living in the home.

Real Estate

There have been many changes when it comes to real estate and buying a home. Every year the real estate market changes, and you never know when the best time is to buy a home. While interest rates are going up, it seems like the homes themselves have come down in price. If you take a look at some years prior, you needed to pounce on a property if you liked it. This year, depending on the property, you can take your time.

If you are unsure whether right now is a good time to buy, take a look at the listings. Some homes can take about two months to sell, but the average home takes about three months, depending on the market. It does not matter how long it takes to sell the home, as the longer it takes, it shows the amount of interest there is in purchasing the home. There are always buyers looking!

There are two terms often used in real estate: Buyer's Market and Seller's Market. A buyer's market occurs when there are more properties available for sale and fewer people looking to buy. A seller's market means there are more people trying to buy a property than there are homes available, so this often leads to multiple buyers interested in the same property.

One metric that is used to help with understanding the market is months of inventory. This tells you how many months it will take to sell the existing listings, assuming no new listings get added. In the City of Toronto on March 15, 2017, that number was an insanely low 0.66 months. In 2019 that number sat at 1.82 months. This means it was still a Seller's market.

We consider it a Seller's market when there are fewer than four months inventory. 4-6 months is a balanced market, and more than six months is a Buyer's market. Properties are staying on the market longer, accepting conditions and not as many are facing multiple offers. So, looking at that, the best time to purchase a property is when there is a buyer's market.

Renting vs Owning Your Home

When you are young and finishing off school, you cannot wait to have your own place and have your own independence, but no one really thinks about the true costs when it comes to renting a home. There are so many factors involved when figuring out the total costs of renting versus owning. Ultimately, you can be paying the same price as far as monthly payments, but what you are getting, when comparing renting and owing, are two very different things.

The cost of renting is ultimately knowing you have to keep paying around the same costs as you would with a mortgage, but you will never actually own the home you are paying to live in. Paying a large amount of rent every month can also make it difficult to break the cycle of renting because you are unable to save enough money to put a down-payment on a mortgage. Some strategic budgeting and planning can help.

When it comes to deciding whether to rent or put a down-payment on a mortgage, it really depends on what your income is, your credit rating, and how much money you have saved. If you are unable to put money down on a mortgage, there are options for you that don't require a down-payment, but you will pay more in the long run. Choosing to go down the route of renting can sometimes be the only option, although it should be considered a short-term or temporary choice. Consider your options, and do not make a decision until you have a plan to cover all the costs that come along with either renting or applying for a mortgage.

Homework

1) What type of mortgage do you have?

2) What the terms of your mortgage? Principal, interest rate, term, Amortization period, a high ratio mortgage (mortgage default insurance) or low ratio mortgage

3) What is your re-payment schedule and renewal date?

4) What are the penalties if you break your mortgage contract early?

5) Do you pay city property tax or additional personal life insurance, disability insurance, or accident and sickness insurance in your mortgage contract?

6) Are you renting? Do you have a budget plan to create a lump sum of money for a down

payment to purchase a property? How long will it take?

OUR LITTLE SECRET

OBSESSIONS

The time making money should be greater than the time that
you are spending money.

- Sophia Amoruso, American Businesswoman

Secret Spending Habits We Enjoy

Everyone has their dirty little secret when it comes to spending money on things they enjoy, but sometimes it can get a little overboard. So, it is time, to be honest with yourself. People spend money on a large variety of things, and there is always something to enjoy spending money on. The top spending habits are food, clothing, cars and entertainment. Do we really realize how much we are spending on those habits and fun activities?

Let's take a look at money wasted on food that is not included in your weekly budget. Most people like to splurge sometimes and go out to a restaurant or drive-thru to get some fast food, but this can add up very quickly if you're not careful. Even buying a little snack at the corner store, or your morning coffee and bagel at Tim Hortons can have you spending at least an extra ten dollars a day. This may seem like a small amount when you look at it each day, but when you total that ten dollars a day to a monthly cost, it's about $300.00 just on unnecessary food and drinks.

One of my clients had a very tight budget and didn't feel she had enough money to purchase groceries. Obviously, she needed to eat, so she purchased a coffee and a muffin from McDonald's every morning for $3, and she would purchase a kid's meal and a coffee for lunch each day for $6. The days that she didn't work, she would also drive to McDonald's because she didn't have groceries in the house.

So, when you add that up and average it over 30 days in a month, she was spending $270/month ($3240/year) just on McDonald's for breakfast and lunch. She was shocked when she recognized it, and we started looking at ways to cut her expenses. She bought a $20 coffee maker and coffee and began spending $4 on a six-pack of fresh-baked muffins each week. She also started buying some groceries, making dinners and taking leftovers for lunch. She was also paying for McDonald's on her credit card, so by cutting out that purchase, she saved on interest rates also.

If you love going to restaurants with the family, well, that is going to cost you money! If you are a 3-4-person family, you could be looking at over $100 for just one meal, when instead, you could spend $100 on your weekly grocery trip. Restaurants are great to go to every once in a while, but going even once a week could be too much. Eating at restaurants is my secret obsession. I love the experience, the atmosphere, the noise, the smells, and especially salivating over the different menu items! So, when I create my budget, I include extra into my eating out budget and remove items like coffee and muffins or clothing purchases. When I review the end of month budget, if I overspent, I make sure to cut back on things for the upcoming month so that I can keep my monthly spending in check.

Do you enjoy going shopping and buying yourself a nice outfit every once in a while? Well, nothing wrong with that, but when it becomes more of a routine than a reward, that can cause you some money issues down the road. Women spend somewhere between $150-$400/month on clothing compared to men. That equals $1800-$4800/year or an average of $125,000 in a lifetime. Even looking at brand name clothing compared to generic clothing brands, there is a huge difference in the cost when the item can look similar.

You can spend $100.00 on a shirt that looks like the same product that is less than half the price. People assume buying a brand name is better because clothing companies spend lots of money on marketing to show the lifestyles of people we want to be like, and this will give the impression that brand name gives you a higher status. If you are insisting on purchasing a specific product, then save for it and watch for when it goes on sale.

There is no reason to pay full price for clothing, as most likely, in a few weeks, it will go on sale and be half the price. Trends change so quickly, so stores are constantly updating their products and changing their prices. Many consignment stores also have high-end clothing but with a lower price tag, and that can also help cut some costs. Most stores have a sale at the end of each season.

What about that vehicle you have? Do you make any small repairs yourself, or do you always bring your car to someone to do it for you? Most people, even for an oil change, will pay for someone else to do something that can be done on their own. This is just throwing money away for no reason. Do you have more than one vehicle, or a habit of buying nice cars that not only cost more, to begin with but will cost more in gas as well?

Have you thought about a vehicle loan versus leasing your vehicle? Both have pros and cons depending on your goals and budget. When you get a vehicle loan, you can consider you "buying" the vehicle, whereas leasing is more like a "rent to own" model. Some of the benefits of buying are that you pay less over the long term, you have the option to sell it, you don't have a mileage limit, and there are no restrictions on the appearance of the vehicle, so if you want to accessorize it, you can.

When you lease a vehicle, you may pay lower monthly payments, but you will have a lump sum purchase price at the end of the term. If you keep the vehicle, you are unable to sell the vehicle, but at the end of the term, you are able to return the vehicle to the dealership. You have a mileage limit and will be charged a fee if you go over it, you may be covered for repair expenses if they are covered by the dealership. I have purchased and leased vehicles over the years, and my personal preference is to buy with a car loan because of the economical advantages, especially at the end of the 4- or 5-year loan; you will no longer have car payments.

Banking is one of those things no one really thinks about, but it can really affect the amount of money you have. Technology has made it, so cash is something we rarely have on hand. Instead, most people will use a credit or debit card to make purchases. It is easier, and you do not have to worry about carrying a bunch of cash on you. The only issue with this is that, unless you are looking at your bank account every day to see the balance, you are not aware of how all those little purchases add up. This makes it more difficult to keep track of your spending.

Your bank will also have monthly fees you have to pay or interest charges if your credit card isn't fully paid off each month. (Remember the Rule of 72, if you aren't paying off your credit card each month and there is an interest rate of 20%, your balance will double every 3 ½ years.) Even using an ATM that isn't at your personal bank will generate extra charges. All of those little fees keep piling up, just for the privilege of having a bank account. Obviously, a bank account is necessary to have, but there are ways to help avoid extra costs.

My recommendation is to spend a couple of weeks tracking all your small expenses, and instead of using a credit card or debit card, you should withdraw that amount to use for the week. This is also a great way to track overspending. If you go through the amount of money you withdrew, then you can decide whether or not to withdraw more or plan better for the next week to reduce overspending.

What about personal women's needs? Women tend to buy a lot more personal products than men; feminine hygiene, makeup, haircare, etc. Not only are women's products normally more expensive than men's, but women have to buy a variety of different products, whereas men need about half the items. If you walk down the personal care aisles, you will see a never-ending number of brands, which can get insanely confusing, and can have you spending a lot more money than you really need to. For example, take a look at makeup and hair products. Hair and makeup trends change as fast as clothing trends, and keeping up with the latest trends can be very expensive. I don't know about you, but most of my makeup and hair trends last longer than a season, so keeping up with the latest changes isn't something I am on top of, but I do see people who do. The changes in colours, lashes, lips, eyebrows, physical body features, long hair/short hair and all the extras can lead to a lot of added expense in your budget.

In regards to entertainment, there are some products that people should consider the risks over reward and look at cutting back on. Lottery tickets, alcohol, and smoking are habits that are unhealthy, and the expense is more than the reward. One of my clients was able to cut down and then quit smoking and instead put money into a jar every time she had a craving. Within the first six months, she had accumulated over $3000, and she was determined to stay smoke-free.

How to Make Those Habits Work for You

All of these habits can really add up if you are not careful. They are all extra costs that are not necessary, and there are other alternatives that can be a better option and save you a lot.

The first spending habit we take a look at is extra food costs, which includes anything that is not on your weekly grocery list. Do you make a weekly grocery list? If you are a coffee drinker and tend to go out to buy your daily coffee even just once a day, that will add up very quickly. Remember, my client who bought McDonald's daily? There are alternatives, though! You can buy a take-out mug and make your coffee from home, which may seem silly because you're still spending the money on both the travel mug and coffee, but it is drastically cheaper than buying a coffee every day.

What about an avid restaurant-goer? If you have a habit of making a weekly trip to your favourite restaurant, then maybe look at a different choice. You could always recreate your favourite restaurant meal in your own home. It will definitely be cheaper, and you will probably have leftovers to eat the next day too. Just because a chef made it, doesn't mean you can't attempt to create the same thing and save a little money while doing so! Cut restaurant outings to once a month and save the money ahead of time, so it is a reward for saving instead of a debt adding up.

Going shopping is another one of those habits that most people enjoy, but some people enjoy it a little too much. Fashion trends constantly change, so there is always something new to buy, even though you already have a full wardrobe of clothing. If you have a spending problem when it comes to buying clothing, start tracking your total costs so you can put into perspective how much you are truly spending each month. It is also a good idea to avoid continually looking at the next new fashion item; there will always be something new, but that doesn't mean you need to have it.

If you really need something, then save for it. If your treat for yourself, is to get an article of clothing once a month, then set aside money for it, and do not go over the amount. Add it to your budget so you are aware of it every month, and do not try to convince yourself to get any more, because financial planning can only do so much. You need to be strong enough to want to make your budget and your finances work for you.

If you have an interest in vehicles, make that work for you instead of work against you. Purchasing another vehicle is a huge cost that doesn't have a good return, and of course, you will need insurance, so your monthly cost will be more. Why not try to fix an old vehicle that needs some work or purchase a vehicle a few years old? Yes, you will still be spending money on a vehicle, but not only will it make you feel proud, but it will also be a lot cheaper compared to buying new.

You really cannot avoid having a bank account these days, but there are ways you can save a little money and avoid those little fees that may come up. Avoid using your bank account for every purchase, and instead, take out a certain amount of cash, and stick to that amount for the week. That way, you know you have not overspent, and you know the total amount left in your bank account. Tracking your weekly spending habits will help you save more money and allow you to easily revaluate each week.

If you are adamant about using your credit card, then stick to that, but do not forget to pay it off regularly. Each day, get into the daily habit of checking what you spent that day and make a payment from your chequing account to your credit card. Interest fees can add up quickly, and there is no need to pay unnecessary charges because you didn't pay off money you know you spent. Do not spend money you do not have.

If there is a large ticket item you want to purchase, plan for it. When do you need to purchase it? How much will it cost, including taxes? What amount can you save weekly? Save for it first, then use your credit card to pay for it. You can get the item you want, but you are also improving your credit by paying off the credit card balance when it is due.

Habits may be hard to break, but it is not impossible to do. As mentioned, it takes hard work and determination to get where you want to be in your life. Many of the habits stated above are so common, yet people do not take notice of them. Change that negative habit into a positive one, so instead of spending money, your habit becomes saving money. Spend some time and write down your habits and how you can make changes so as not to break the bank. Stop throwing your money away at unnecessary products and purchases, and use that money to invest, or build up your credit.

Find your motivation to break through those habits and start saving up that money again. Remember, you can always go back to some of the things you really love, but be realistic about what your priorities are and what your future looks like. You are probably like the majority of my clients; you are reading this because you need some help figuring out how to secure your future.

Homework

1) What is your credit score? www.creditkarma.com
2) What are your largest spending habits? Hint, it may be what costs you less, but you purchase most often. Take a look at your weekly tracking sheets.
3) What purchases over $100 do you need to purchase in the next three months, six months, one year? A) How much does it cost with taxes? B) Break it down to a daily saving amount?
4) What changes can you make to your current spending habits?

JENNIFER WOODBECK

YOU CAN DO IT ... I BELIEVE IN YOU!

When you are passionate about something NO ONE will get in your way.

Let's Review

Yahoo! Congratulations! Bravo! You've done it. You've read all the chapters, done all the homework, and you are on your way to financial freedom. I am so proud of you!

I am dedicating this chapter to you, whether you are single, married, separated, divorced, widowed or it's complicated, you are amazing and brave to me. My financial journey has had lots of ups and downs, but I know through strategies and dedication to learning, I have been able to stay on track and continue to go upwards now.

So, now that you have read all the steps to being financially stable let's go out there and make it all happen. Having your tailored financial plan can not only decrease your overall stress but can also help you create the life you have always wanted for yourself and your family. Tracking your spending and creating habits that can get you to save money early on will have you in a much more stable place financially compared to making your financial plan later on in life. As women, we are able to build our credit on our own, and buy the things we want in life, so let's take advantage of this!

Looking back not even eighty years ago, the world was a very different place, and women did not have nearly as many rights as we do now. We used to go from our parent's home to our husband's home, and never had any sense of personal finance. Things have come a long way, and it's important that all women know how to properly take care of themselves when it comes to finances and saving money. Every woman has an opportunity to make an amazing future for herself, which is definitely a great change in our society.

Start easy and track your income and spending so you can see what needs to be tweaked. Overspending is a major reason why people do not have extra money in their pockets. Do not spend money you do not have, especially on things you do not need! If you are able to see exactly what you are spending money on, then you can start evaluating your needs and decide if certain purchases are necessary. Once you have this organized, create a budget for yourself, and stick to it.

Many people create budgets, but few people actually stick to them, and that can make a huge difference in your ability to save. Review the chapter on budgeting, *the "B" word is NOT a bad word*. Budgeting may seem like an overwhelming task, but it exists to help you set goals for yourself. Families or individuals that are financially stable have a budget and follow it, and you can too!

As you now know, budgets are not the only way to increase your income. There is no need to worry; remember the rule of 72 and just start investing so you can have a constant inflow of money. There are endless options when it comes to ways of investing, so find what works for you and your budget; it's that simple.

Life is too short to keep procrastinating about when is a good time to be financially stable. Compound interest works in your favour the earlier you start. Avoid waiting until you are close to retirement; do it as early as possible so you feel comfortable that when retirement comes around, you are fully prepared and can live a relaxing, stress-free rest of your life.

Why wait until the last minute to get your finances sorted out when you can start making it happen today? If you have debts, write down a financial plan to get them paid off, and if you are unsure, there are financial advisors to help you at every turn. My recommendation is to pay off the debts that have an interest rate above 6% because if you have investments, they should be earning you about 6% minimum, so at least your money is somewhat balanced.

Having debt can really put a damper on your attempt to build your credit up and save your money. Not only will the original debt add stress to your life, but the interest rates will keep going up, and you will have to keep paying that interest until your debt is paid off. Set a plan to eliminate all your debt, so you can work towards saving money and enjoying life. I believe anyone has the opportunity to make it happen and create the best life for themselves, and I believe it can happen for you as well!

Student debts are one of those things that many people choose not to pay off right away. Considering there are options to defer your payment until you are more financially sound, why would you feel the need to pay it off immediately? Well, even though interest does not normally build up when you defer your student loans, you are still avoiding payment and stalling when you could work towards getting them paid off as quickly as possible. There is no reason to hold onto that debt if you have the ability to make the payments.

It isn't just avoiding paying off your debt that will bring down your credit score; it is also missing regular payments on credit cards, loans or other bills. Just try to remember, if you made a purchase, make sure at the end of the month that it is paid off. Always have that money put aside, so you know you are able to pay off any credit cards or loans at the end of the month. If you have a payment plan, avoid missing a payment as this can eventually affect your chances of having good, stable credit.

Your financial goals are important to me, and I am

sure that no matter what your financial goals are, you need to make a plan and follow through. If you have plans to purchase a house, figure out the steps, such as time frame, down payment and credit score, to reach that goal. Rushing into something, especially when finances are involved, can be incredibly overwhelming, so take your time and don't rush; you will get there. Having a plan makes it easier to track and also helps you see that you can succeed in life if you truly want to.

Lastly, you want to make sure to eliminate all your bad habits. They are not helping you or your financial goals in any way. Focus on your goals first; new trends and technology will always come around, but your future is worth avoiding those unnecessary purchases. If your financial plan gets in the way of purchases you'd like to make, then make those purchases later in life. Once you are financially sound, your options are endless!

These tips can get you far, but you should want the best life for yourself so you can reach your dreams and goals while you continue to be strong and stick to your plan and budget. Your passion for your dreams and goals will help you stay on target. I believe that your dreams should be obtainable and should make you excited. When you want your dreams enough, you are able to prioritize and able to turn off all the thoughts in your head that say, "I need to buy this item" or "I need to spend money on this."

Truthfully, you may think at the time you need it, but a bright, stress-free future seems like it is definitely worth avoiding that new pair of shoes! If you really want the shoes, consider the number of hours of work needed to purchase that item and decide if the cost is a good balance. Or, instead of the immediate purchase, save the money first and then look at them as a reward for achieving a certain goal. There is no problem with rewarding yourself for something good; just avoid making it a routine. Instead, focus on your dreams and put money towards making your dream a reality.

Your Relationship with Money

If you believe you have a negative relationship with money, you are not the odd one out. Many people, at least sometime in their life, believe they are making the wrong decisions when it comes to how they are spending their money and where it's going. A healthy relationship with money takes a lot of effort, time, and planning; there is no way to get where you want financially overnight, but you can get there.

Many people continue this unhealthy relationship with money because they are stuck in the same routine, and have not changed their attitude or perspective. If you believe you will always be in debt, or constantly trying to catch up on bills, then that is where you will stay. You have to want something better for yourself to make it happen. Let's change that unhealthy relationship with money into a positive one, and you will have no regrets!

If you want to change your relationship with money, you have to change the way you think and look at it. If you have been overly negative about money, or the lack of it, change how you talk to yourself about it. Stop telling yourself, "I will always be in debt," or "My money problems are here to stay," or "I can't afford it," as this never helps anything. Instead, you need to be telling yourself positive affirmations each day when it comes to money.

Putting yourself down will not help anything; make yourself feel good for the positive changes you are making in your life. Check my website for money affirmations. Once you have made a list of your dreams and goals add them into your daily affirmations. The one I use often with my clients is "Every day I am attracting more and more money. I am so happy and grateful that I can ……… My Finances improve beyond my dreams."

Firstly, stop blaming yourself for not making the right choices in your life. I believe the choices you have made in life may have stalled you from getting on the right path, but they have not stopped you from having a strong financial future. Stop telling yourself you are not where you want to be because of your education, your intelligence, or your background. It does not matter where you came from; it matters what your dreams and goals are and where you plan on going. You can make it happen!

Many people spend so much time blaming their financial situation on something else, but ultimately, they are the only ones who have the power to change it. It does not matter whether you want to change something financially or personally in your life; whether you believe you can or you believe you can't, you are right! This is where you need to have the strength to ignore all those negative feelings you have towards money and turn them into positive emotions. Tell yourself you will be financially stable; if you want something badly enough, you have the ability to make it happen.

Just like any relationship, our bodies and minds will tell us if something is off. If your relationship with money is considered a negative one, then ask yourself why that is. Do you find yourself having health issues because of it? With any type of relationship, if something is not right or in place, it takes a toll on how you feel about yourself and how your body feels in general. If you have money troubles, your stress is going to skyrocket, and you are going to feel like you are trapped. Getting out of that mindset can be the best thing for you and your relationship with money.

Lastly, you want to treat your relationship with

money, like any other relationship in your life. You need to give it love, or that relationship will not grow. As silly as it may sound to be comparing a relationship with money to a relationship with a person, it is true. You need to give it respect and make time for it so that your money can actually grow. You need to be able to see both the good and bad, but do not bring yourself down if you made a financial mistake; learn from it so you can grow from it. This type of relationship takes time and effort, but if you truly put in the work, it will pay off in time.

Have faith in yourself, and believe you can make the best life for you and your family. See what changes you need to make and get started, and very quickly, you will see a positive change in yourself and your lifestyle in general. Even better, you will see a change in your finances, and you will be wondering why you didn't get started even sooner!

Important Money Makeover Strategies

Now that you have all the in-depth strategies let's sum it up with a quick recap. Essentially there are six steps to financial independence to create the new you.

1.   Cash Flow

There are many ways to change your cash flow. One way is to budget. Budgets can help you understand and track your financial situation, cut back on non-necessity items, and control your spending. Another way is to increase your cash flow. There is a large demand for online services and on-demand services such as ride-sharing, accommodations, dog walking, babysitting, freelancers, and more.

Consider turning your passion into a business either through leveraging your professional expertise in freelance projects or by selling the things you make. Adding an income to your life, even just for a temporary period of time, will help you wipe out debt or increase your lifestyle for the better.

2. Debt Management

Have you had the chance to crush a final debt payment, meet a savings goal, purchase a large item for cash instead of credit because you saved for it? The largest and most complicated financial issue is consumer debt. Credit cards have one of the largest interest rates and also one of the easiest forms of accumulating debt quickly. Even adding an extra $10 to what you currently pay onto a debt will save you months of interest. The Rule of 72 will show you how interest will work for you or against you.

For example, an average credit card interest rate of 19.99% will double your debt over 3 ½ years. So, your $10,000 owed today will be $20,000 in 3 ½ years. It is always best to pay high-interest debts first and make sure you pay extra payments and not just the interest or minimum payment amount.

3.   Proper Protection

Life insurance is one of the most important components of a strong financial future. If you are no longer around, your family will be left with your debt, your final expenses, and also the loss of your income. The basic rule is 10-20 times your annual income depending on your debt amount if you have children and any additional income from a spouse.

Life insurance isn't the only way to protect your wealth; it is very important to have critical illness insurance and disability insurance. If you don't have critical illness insurance then you will need to use your savings or retirement plan in order to pay for expenses while you are ill. Similarly, if you don't have disability insurance and become injured, you may not receive an income while you recover from your injury.

4.   Build Wealth

Wealth building can mean many things, but essentially, the focus is to save, keep up with or stay above inflation, and reduce taxes. The basic wealth formula is Money + Time +/- Rate of Return-Inflation-tax=Wealth. The formula may appear straightforward, but making your money work for you can be complicated.

Keep in mind; your money will do what you tell it to; remember the rule of 72. If your money is in an investment account at 1% interest, it will take 72 years to double. The road to $1 Million at retirement is easier the earlier you start. If you are 25 years old and save $655.30/month, you will reach your goal in 40 years, but if you wait until you are 45 years old, you will need to save $2432.89/month; this is based on a 5% tax-deferred account such as a TFSA.

5.   Emergency Fund

Having an emergency fund should not include using credit cards or payday loans. Building a reserve is very important to have for unexpected expenses. Even having $1000 in an account is a simple but effective strategy to ensure some peace of mind, but the goal is to have 3-6 months of expenses in an emergency fund. I recommend having your insurance protection in place before focusing on your emergency fund because the devastation of a lifelong injury or illness causes more damage to your family.

6.   Estate Preservation

At the end of the day, you may have everything in your financial house in place and be on the road to financial freedom for you and your family, but do you have a will? Only about 50% of Canadian adults have estate preservation, such as a will or living trust. Unfortunately, if you don't have a will, your family runs the risk of having your estate settled in courts and possibly losing lots of what you worked so hard to preserve.

Resources to empower your belief in yourself

I believe in you! It is often hard to believe in yourself from time to time, but you have picked up this book for a reason, searching for a resource to get on a path to a better financial future. I will say it loud and clear ... I believe in you!

There are a few different ways in which people learn; visually, audibly, verbally, or physically. Find out which type you are and then see which resource works for you. Some of my favourite visual books include:

1) *#Maxout Your Life: Strategies for becoming an elite performer*, by Ed Mylett

2) *How to Rewrite Reality: Becoming the author of the stories in your life*, by Shiraz

3)   *Girl, Stop Apologizing: A Shame-free plan for embracing and achieving your goal*, by Rachel Hollis

Some of my favourite Audible or verbal books include:

1)   https://simonsinek.com/

2)   *Unshakeable*, by Tony Robbins

3)   *Nice girls still don't get the corner office: Unconscious mistakes women make to sabotage their careers*, by Lois P. Frankel, PhD

If you are looking for a more physical way of learning, then consider how you have been feeling and thinking about your life. What has triggered you to feel this way, good or bad, and how can you make changes? Tapping into those physical feelings will help you stay on top of your goals and dreams and get into a physical place that you are consistently feeling good with less stress, better sleep, and a lighter step each day.

There will be days when you feel unsure of yourself, but that is where a financial planner is here to help. There are so many resources out there; you just need to do the research, and if you really want to be financially stable, you will do what it takes.

ABOUT THE AUTHOR

"Life is too short to say 'no' to an opportunity. Always say 'yes,' then figure it out."

Jennifer Woodbeck is the consummate financial professional. Not only does she provide the full spectrum of financial products and services, as well as knowledgeable advice, she is also an in-demand speaker and a published author. Jennifer is your Friendly Finance Coach, based in Mississauga, Ontario, and has clients throughout North America.

Jennifer was born and raised in Thunder Bay, Ontario. She has a large, close-knit extended family and had a lot of strong, determined female role models in her life. Growing up, she was outgoing, making friends easily, and she participated in a lot of sports and activities, from basketball and freestyle skiing to jazz and tap dancing. She was a good student and liked school, which has led to a lifelong love of learning.

Highly driven, whether in sports or academically, Jennifer fast-tracked her high school diploma, completing the five-year program in four years by taking summer and evening classes, as well as supplemental classes instead of a lunch break. She didn't know why she was so driven to achieve; she just felt she didn't have a ceiling, that she could always do better and go bigger. She wanted to be a teacher when she graduated and completed her qualifications as an

Early Childhood Educator before she was 20, but after two years in the workforce, she realized she wasn't ready for a career just yet, so she returned to school. She had always enjoyed science and math, so she enrolled at Lakehead University in Thunder Bay, in their Honours Biology program. She wasn't sure what she was going to do with her degree at first, but after hearing about it as an interesting career opportunity, she applied for a diploma program in Respiratory Therapy. After completing the entrance exams, she was accepted into the program after the first year of her Bachelor's studies (instead of with her full degree). After completing her education and internships in Toronto, and graduating with a Diploma in Respiratory Therapy, she worked at Sick Kids Hospital, then Mount Sinai.

After 11 years in Toronto, Jennifer was given the opportunity to return to Thunder Bay to build and open a COPD education clinic from the ground up, creating programs, and developing systems for patient management. Not one to shy away from a challenge, she researched what was needed, using all available resources, and served as a COPD Educator and Respiratory Therapist there until 2017. During her years in healthcare, always striving for the next goal, Jennifer went back to school and completed a BA (2016) with a focus on business management and nursing courses at Lakehead University.

Jennifer started looking for a change when modifications to the healthcare system started making it more challenging and less rewarding to work in the field. The idea of working in finance and insurance appealed to her, having seen first-hand the devastation families endured when their insurance coverage wasn't sufficient to meet long-term needs after the death or disability of a loved one. April 1, 2017 was her red-letter day, marking the day she left healthcare to become a financial professional and insurance broker at World Financial Group in Thunder Bay. She switched from working to improve health to working to improve financial health. The empathy that always drove her working as an RT has now been directed towards her clients, striving to provide them with the products they need to serve their best interests. Her experiences with the difficult parts of patient care have given her the skill set necessary to have the difficult conversations about death and disability with her clients sympathetically and compassionately.

As a financial professional with World Financial Group, a full-service brokerage, Jennifer offers and advises on a full range of products and services offered by over 50 financial services companies. Her services include Retirement Planning, Debt Management; Budgeting; Savings and Investments; all types of Insurance products and coverage; Estate Planning; and Tax strategies. Her particular focus is currently on insurance coverage and ensuring her clients will be financially stable in the event of unexpected healthcare challenges. After her years in the medical field, she understands that not everything is covered when a medical emergency arises, and the financial repercussions can be long-lasting.

Expanding on her work in financial services, Jennifer has turned to the idea of educating people on the importance of managing their financial picture. To that end, she works one-on-one with her clients, doing regular check-ins on their current situations and managing any changes as they arise. She is also doing webinars and speaking at events in the US and Canada and is currently developing an 8-week course to accompany *Butterflies and Shiny Things: A Women's Guide on How to Manage Financial Distractions*, which takes a more in-depth look at the topics covered in the book. She is also a speaker at community events, tailoring her topics to the audience she is addressing. In the past, she has presented to business people, women's groups, tradespeople (about extra-union investing), and the Indigenous populations in Northern Ontario.

Jennifer is married to Patrick, an air ambulance paramedic, and has two sons. They also have a cat and a dog. Jennifer and her family relocated to Mississauga, Ontario, in early 2019. Always up for a challenge and new experiences, in her career and her family life, they are an outdoorsy family, enjoying skiing, hiking, and all the lake activities, like swimming, kayaking, and boating. Her love of adventure is also reflected in her down-time activities, with action and superhero movies being family favourites. She prefers podcasts to reading, and she loves remodelling.

"Change is good. Just have a plan."

JENNIFER WOODBECK